KETO DIET COOKBOOK For Beginners #2019

700+ Simple, Quick and Easy Recipes for Busy People on Keto Diet with 21-Day Meal Plan (Keto Diet for Beginners)

Sabella Wilson

Table Of Contents

Description

We each have a human body that's run on fuel. Are you going to get your fuel from carbohydrates and continue to go through blood sugar cycles that also cause you to gain weight?

Or, are you going to make the commitment to be in the ketosis metabolic state? Like a happy marriage, it's a commitment that gives you back far more than it takes! It'll give you a slimmer, trimmer body. It will give you better health. It will give you so much more energy, because you won't feel sluggish or stuck in a carb coma cycle. It will give you back the person that you have always dreamed you could be. When you continue to eat a moderate or high carbohydrate diet, you're not just enjoying sugar, you are keeping yourself further and further away from the kind of body that you want. The kind of body that prompted you to pick up this book.

But, when you go into a ketosis metabolic state? That is when real results happen. Many Keto Dieters are shocked when the pounds start to quickly drop off. But that is what you should expect when you switch metabolic states. You are struggling to burn the existing weight, not burn the fuel from what you just ate at breakfast this morning. Ketosis is the state which burns your existing weight.

This book presents you the following healthy, easy and quick to make recipes:

Breakfast

Lunch

Dinner

Smoothies

Soups

Fat Bombs

Salads

Sauces And Dressing

Dessert

Appetizer & Snacks

Soups, Broth & Stews

Sounds good to be true? Let's get to the facts and prove the benefits to you. Click add to cart and start a helathy journey! That number on the scale just keeps getting lighter and lighter.

Introduction

When you start learning how to drive, you won't immediately know how to overtake, change lanes, and the uses of the devices in the car, how to reverse, and even to hit the horn. Everything is one after the other. Like I said earlier, "the journey of a thousand miles begins with a step." It is one step after the other and this book will help and guide you through this journey.

It has been a great pleasure for us to impart and flash the torch which points out the way to you. We are delighted that this book of ours has been a tool in modifying your life and taking you across the finish line of that journey of a thousand miles.

The ketogenic diet, if not the best, is one of the best ways in reducing body weight and excess fat. It was designed for the treatment of seizures, but unknown to mankind; it is like an onion of blessings. Within it, there are a lot of benefits and layers of treatment. It has been tested and trusted by many scientists all over the world.

Thanks for downloading this book. It's my firm belief that it will provide you with all the answers to your questions. Let the ketogenic diet be a part of you because the ketogenic diet is not a diet, it is a lifestyle!

Show the world the lifestyle! Happy reading!!

Breakfast

1. Red Pepper, Mozzarella and Bacon Frittata

Prep Time: 35 MIN
Serve: 6
Ingredients:

- 1 tbsp olive oil
- 7 slices bacon
- 1 red bell pepper, chopped
- ¼ cup heavy cream
- ¼ cup parmesan cheese, grated
- 9 eggs
- Salt and pepper
- 2 tbsp parsley, chopped
- 4 cups Bella mushrooms, large
- ½ cup basil, chopped
- 4 oz mozzarella cheese, cubed
- 2 oz goat cheese, chopped

Directions:

1. Set oven to 350 F.
2. Heat olive oil in a skillet then add bacon and cook for 5 minutes until browned.
3. Add red pepper and cook for 2 minutes until soft. While pepper cooks, add cream, parmesan cheese, eggs, parsley, salt, and pepper to a bowl and whisk to combine.

1. Add mushrooms to pot, stir and cook for 5 minutes until soaked in fat. Add basil, cook for 1 minute then

add mozzarella.

4. Add in egg mixture and use a spoon to move ingredients around so that the egg gets on the bottom of the pan.
5. Top with goat cheese and place in oven for 8 minutes then broil for 6 minutes.
6. Use a knife to pry frittata edges from pan and place on a plate and slice.

Calories 408
Total Fats 31.2g
Net Carbs: 2.4g
Protein 19.2g
Fiber: 0.8g

2. Cheese and Sausage Pies

Prep Time: 40 MIN
Serve: 2

Ingredients:

- 1 ½ pieces chicken sausage
- ½ tsp rosemary
- ¼ tsp baking soda
- ¼ cup coconut flour
- ¼ tsp cayenne pepper
- 1/8 tsp salt
- 5 egg yolks
- 2 tsp lemon juice
- ¼ cup coconut oil
- 2 tbsp coconut milk
- ¾ cheddar cheese, grated

Directions:

1. Set oven to 350 F.
2. Chop sausage, heat skillet and cook sausage. While sausages cook combine all dry ingredients in a bowl. In another bowl combine egg yolks, lemon juice, oil and coconut milk. Add liquids to dry mixture and add ½ cup of cheese; fold to combine and put into 2 ramekins.
3. Add cooked sausages to the batter and use a spoon to push into the mixture.
2. Bake for 25 minutes until golden on top. Top with leftover cheese and broil for 4 minutes.

4. Serve warm.

Calories 711
Total Fats 65.3g
Net Carbs: 5.8g
Protein 34.3g
Fiber: 11.5g

3. Breakfast Quiche

Prep Time: 30 MIN
Serve: 2

Ingredients:

- 3 tbsp coconut oil
- 5 eggs
- 8 slices bacon, cooked and chopped
- ½ cup cream
- 2 cups baby spinach, roughly chopped
- 1 cup red pepper, chopped
- 1 cup yellow onion, chopped
- 2 cloves garlic, minced
- 1 cup mushrooms, chopped
- 1 cup cheddar cheese, grated
- Salt

Directions:

1. Preheat oven to 375 F.
2. In a large bowl, mix all vegetables including the mushrooms together.
3. In another small bowl, whisk the 5 eggs with the cream
4. Carefully scoop the veggie mixture into a muffin pan coated with cooking spray, top with egg and cheese filling up to ¾ of the muffin tins. Sprinkle with chopped bacon on top.

5. Place in the oven to bake for 15 minutes or until the top of the quiche are firm.
6. Let it cool for a few minutes before serving.

Calories 210
Total Fats 13g
Net Carbs: 5g
Protein 6g

4. Chicharrones con Huevos Pork Rind and Eggs

Prep Time: 30 MIN
Serve: 3

Ingredients:

- 4 slices bacon
- 1.5 oz pork rinds
- 1 avocado, cubed
- ¼ cup onion, chopped
- 1 tomato, chopped
- 2 jalapeno pepper, seeds removed and chopped
- 5 eggs
- ¼ cup cilantro
- Salt and pepper

Directions:

1. Heat skillet and cook bacon until slightly crisp. Remove from pot and put aside on paper towels.
2. Add pork rinds to the pot along with onion, tomatoes, pepper and cook for 3 minutes until onions are soft and clear.
3. Add cilantro, stir together gently and add eggs. Scramble eggs and then add avocado and fold.
4. Serve.

Calories 508
Total Fats 43g
Net Carbs: 12g
Protein 5g
Fiber: 5.3g

5. Raspberry & Cacao Breakfast Bowl

Prep Time: 40 MIN
Serve: 1

Ingredients:

- 1 cup almond milk
- 1 tbsp cacao powder
- 3 tbsp chia seeds
- ¼ cup raspberry
- 1 tsp agave or xylitol

Directions:

1. In a small bowl, combine the almond milk and cocoa powder. Stir well.
2. Add the chia seeds to the bowl and let it rest for 5 minutes.
3. Using a fork, fluff the chia and cacao mixture and then place in the fridge to chill for at least 30 minutes.
4. Serve with raspberries and a drizzle of agave on top

Calories 230
Total Fats 20g
Net Carbs: 4g
Protein 15g

6. Anaheim pepper Gruyere Waffles

Prep Time: 16 MIN
Serve: 2

Ingredients:

- 1 small Anaheim pepper
- 3 eggs
- 1/4 cup cream cheese
- 1/4 cup Gruyere cheese
- 1 tbsp coconut flour
- 1 tsp Metamucil powder
- 1 tsp baking powder
- Salt and pepper to taste

Directions:

1. In a blender, mix together all ingredients except for the cheese and Anaheim pepper. Once the ingredients are mixed well, add cheese and pepper. Blend well until all ingredients are mix well.
2. Heat your waffle iron; pour on the waffle mix and cook 5-6 minutes. Serve hot.

Calories 223.55
Total Fats 17g
Net Carbs: 5.50g
Protein 11g

7. Nutty Cocoa Cereal

Prep Time: 12 MIN
Serve: 2

Ingredients:

- 3 tsp organic butter
- ¾ cup toasted walnuts, roughly chopped
- ¾ cup toasted macadamia nuts, roughly chopped
- ½ cup coconut shreds, unsweetened
- ½ tbsp stevia optional
- 2 cups almond milk
- 1/8 tsp salt

Directions:

1. Melt the butter in a pot over the medium heat. Add the toasted nuts to the pot and stir for 2 minutes.
2. Add the shredded coconut into the pot and continue stirring to make sure to not burn the ingredients.
3. Drizzle with stevia if usingand then pour the milk into the pot. Add salt. Stir again and turn the heat off.
4. Allow resting for 10 minutes to allow the ingredients to soak in the milk before serving.

Calories 515
Total Fats 50.3g
Net Carbs: 14.4g
Protein 6.5g
Fiber: 7.3g

8. Egg Muffin Cups

Prep Time: 30 min

Serves 6

Ingredients:

- 6 Eggs
- 1/2 cup of Sliced Spinach
- 6 slices of Shaved Nitrate Free Turkey
- Light Mozzarella Cheese
- 2 tablespoons of Red Onion
- 3 tablespoons of Red Pepper
- Fresh Pepper
- Salt
- Olive Oil Spray
- Fresh Basil optional

Directions:

1. Preheat your oven to 350 degrees.
2. Slice your spinach, grate your mozzarella cheese and prepare your red onion and red pepper.
3. Get a nonstick muffin tin and spray with olive oil.
4. Place turkey in one of the muffin tin cups. Make sure it's resting both on the sides and bottom of your tin.
5. Crack 1 egg and pour into your newly made turkey cup. Repeat this with each egg into it's own cup.
6. Add some spinach, red pepper, cheese, and red onion on top of each egg.

7. Season each egg with salt and fresh pepper. Can also add basil if you're using it.
8. Place your tin into the oven and continue to bake till your eggs are all set and their whites are an opaque color. Should be about 10 minutes to get a runnier yolk and around 15 minutes if you want a harder yolk. Be aware that each egg muffin will continue cooking for a short time after they've left the oven.
9. Serve and Enjoy!

Nutrition Value per serving: 1 Egg Muffin Cup.

9 g of Protein.

6 g of Fat.

2 g of Carbs.

95 Calories.

9. Perfected Scrambled Eggs

Serves 2

Ingredients:

- 6 Eggs
- 2 tablespoons of Sour Cream
- 2 tablespoons of Butter
- 1/2 teaspoon of Salt
- 4 strips of Bacon
- 1/2 teaspoon of Onion Powder
- 1/2 teaspoon of Garlic Powder
- 1/4 teaspoon of Black Pepper
- 1/4 teaspoon of Paprika

Directions:

1. Crack your eggs in an ungreased, cold pan and then add your butter. Wait to mix eggs till you put the heat on. Don't season the eggs until after cooked it will break them down and make them watery instead of creamy.
2. Put your pan on medium-high heat. Start stirring the butter and eggs together using preferably a silicone spatula. While stirring your eggs, cook some bacon strips in a different pan to your desired level of crispiness.
3. Alternate stirring your eggs both on heat and off the heat. A few seconds on and a few seconds off the flame. If the eggs begin cooking in a thin, dry

looking layer at the bottom of your pan, take if off heat. Scrape it using your spatula and that thin layer should regain some of its creaminess.

4. Once the eggs are almost done turn off the flame. Your eggs will cook a little more due to residual heat in your pan.
5. Add 2 tablespoons of your sour cream. Season your eggs using the pepper, salt, paprika, onion powder, and garlic powder.
6. You can add in a couple stalks of chopped green onion for some contrasting flavor.
7. Serve and Enjoy!

Nutrition Value per serving:

25 g of Protein.

35 g of Fat.

2 g of Carbs.

444 Calories.

10. Deep Fried Eggs

1 Serving

Ingredients:

- 2 Eggs
- 3 slices of Bacon

Directions:

1. Heat oil in your deep fryer to approximately 375 degrees.
2. Cook your bacon.
3. Crack eggs into your prep bowl.
4. Slip egg into the center of your fryer. Don't drop eggs in, try to slip the eggs in near the surface.
5. Using two different spatulas, corral your egg into a ball. This may take a little practice to get the hang of.
6. Fry for approximately 3-4 minutes or until bubbling stops.
7. Drain on paper towels.
8. Serve and Enjoy!

Nutrition Value per serving:

27 g of Protein.

24 g of Fat.

1 gram of Carbs.

321 Calories.

11. Steak & Eggs

Serves 1

Ingredients:

- 3 Eggs
- 1 tablespoon of Butter
- 4 ounces of Sirloin
- 1/4 of an Avocado
- Pepper
- Salt

Directions:

1. Melt butter in your pan. Fry the eggs until whites have been set and yolk is done to your desired preference. Season them with pepper and salt.
2. Cook sirloin in another pan until desired preference. Slice into small strips and season with pepper and salt.
3. Slice up avocado and add to your dish.
4. Serve and Enjoy!

Nutrition Value per serving:

44 g of Protein.

26 g of Fat.

3 g of Net Carbs.

510 Calories.

12. Scotch Eggs

Serves 4

Ingredients:

- 4 large Eggs
- 8 slices of Thick Cut Bacon
- 12 ounce package of Jimmy Dean's Pork Sausage
- 4 Toothpicks

Directions:

1. Hard boil your eggs.
2. Peel your eggs. Let them dry and cool off.
3. Split your sausage equally into four parts. Pat down each of these parts into a circle.
4. Place egg in each of these circles and wrap it with your sausage. Adjust your sausage so that your eggs are covered completely.
5. Refrigerate them for between approximately 30 to 60 minutes.
6. Form a cross out of two pieces of your bacon.
7. Place your wrapped egg in the center of the cross and fold your bacon over the egg. Use a toothpick to secure it together.
8. Repeat this process on all 4 eggs.
9. Cook eggs in a 450 degree convection oven for approximately 20 minutes. Regular ovens can work but it might need to be finished off using a broiler.
10. Eggs are done when your bacon is nice and crisp.
11. Serve and Enjoy!

Nutritional Value - Serving Size 1 Scotch Egg:

25 g of Protein.

33 g of Fat.

2 g of Carbs.

405 Calories.

13. One Skillet Eggs & Bacon

Ingredients:

- 4 large Eggs
- 8 slices of Bacon
- 1 tablespoon of Butter
- 1/2 cup of Chopped Cauliflower or Broccoli
- 1/2 cup of Finely Chopped Celery
- 1 Peeled Carrot
- 1/2 cup of Shredded Colby Jack Cheese
- 1/2 of a large Chopped White Onion.

Directions:

1. Slice your bacon across its grain into smaller strips.
2. Melt butter in a large sized skillet over medium heat.
3. Add your bacon and vegetables.
4. Stir often and saute your vegetables and bacon in the butter approximately 20 minutes. You want the bacon to start crisping on its edges and you want the vegetables to being caramelizing.
5. Spread your mixture over your skillet as evenly as possible and make four wells one in each quarter of the skillet.
6. Break an egg into each of the wells. Cook eggs until nearly done. Cook shorter if you like your yolks runny and longer if you like them harder.
7. When eggs are nearly done sprinkle cheese on top and let cook until cheese melts and eggs are done.
8. Serve and Enjoy!

14. Ricotta Scrambled Eggs

Serves 1

Ingredients:

- 2 Eggs
- 150 g of 2% Fat Ricotta Cheese
- 50 g of Italian Dry Salami
- 1 teaspoon of Rosemary
- 1 tablespoon of Olive Oil
- Pepper
- Salt

Directions:

1. Chop your salami up into smaller cubes. Fry them together in a small pan using olive oil.
2. While frying, whisk your eggs, add pepper, rosemary, and salt.
3. Add your ricotta into egg mixture, mix well to break up any big lumps.
4. Add your eggs and ricotta mixture to the pan and cook for approximately 5 minutes until done.
5. Serve and Enjoy!

Nutrition Value per serving:

28 g of Protein.

45 g of Fat.

5 g of Carbs.

598 Calories.

15. Clouds of Eggs

Serves 4

Ingredients:

- 4 large Eggs
- 2 slices of Bacon
- 2 tablespoons of Parmesan Cheese
- Pepper
- Salt
- Onion Powder
- Garlic Powder

Directions:

1. Split your egg yolks from your egg whites.
2. Cut up bacon and cook for some bacon bits.
3. Put your eggs in a bowl and then whip them till they are stiff.
4. Shred your parmesan cheese into your egg whites and then add in bacon bits.
5. Split your egg white into four separate mounds on parchment paper or a silicon mat.
6. Bake your egg whites for 5 minutes at approximately 350 degrees until they are set.
7. Put egg yolk into each of your mounds.
8. Bake your egg whites until brown.
9. Serve and Enjoy!

Nutritional Value - Serving Size 1 Egg:

6 g of Protein.

7 g of Fat.

1 gram of Carb.

98 Calories.

Lunch

16. Fantastic Lemon Thyme Chicken:

Nutrition Value per serving:

Serves: 4
Calories: 120
Fat: 8 g
Protein: 12 g
Carbohydrates: 1 gram

Ingredients:

- 10-15 cloves of garlic
- 2 sliced lemons
- ½ teaspoon of ground pepper
- 1 teaspoon of thyme
- 3 ½ -pound whole chicken

Directions:

1. Arrange the lemon and garlic on the base of a slow cooker.
2. Mix the spices together and use them to season the chicken.
3. Put the chicken in the slow cooker.
4. Cover and cook on low for 4 hours.
5. Remove the chicken; let it stand for 15 minutes and the serve.

17. Mackerel, Spinach, Arugula, Cherry Tomatoes, Olive Oil, Rice Vinegar and Lemon Juice:

Nutrition Value per serving:

Serves: 4
Calories: 287.0
Fat: 4.6 g
Sodium: 589 milligram
Protein: 27.4 g
Carbohydrates: 3.2 g

Ingredients:

- 2 cups canned mackerel, drained
- ¼ cup olive oil
- ¼ cup rice vinegar
- 1 tablespoon lemon juice
- 1 tablespoon fresh dill
- ½ teaspoon salt
- 1 teaspoon black pepper
- 4 cups fresh spinach
- 2 cups arugula
- 1 cup cherry tomatoes, halved

Directions:

1. In a blow combine the olive oil, vinegar, lemon juice, dill, salt and black pepper to make a dressing. Whisk until well blended.
2. In another bowl combine the spinach and arugula. Drizzle the dressing over the greens and toss to coat. Reserve a little of the dressing to drizzle over the mackerel, if desired.
3. Transfer the green mixture to serving plates and top with the mackerel, cherry tomatoes and additional dressing if desired.

18. Gorgeous Coconut Turmeric Pork Curry:

Nutrition Value per serving:

Serves: 4
Calories: 425
Fat: 31 g
Protein: 30 g
Carbohydrates: 7 g

Ingredients:

- pounds of cubed pork shoulder
- 1 tablespoon of coconut oil
- 1 tablespoon of olive oil
- 1 diced yellow onion
- 2 cloves of minced garlic
- 2 tablespoon of tomato paste
- 1 can of coconut milk, 12 ounces
- 1 cup of water
- ½ cup white wine
- 1 teaspoon of turmeric
- 1 teaspoon of curry powder
- ½ teaspoon of paprika
- Salt and pepper

Directions:

1. Heat 1 tablespoon of olive oil in a saucepan and sauté the garlic and onions for 3 minutes.
2. Add the pork and brown it and then add the tomato paste.

3. Mix the remaining ingredients in the crock pot and then add the pork.
4. Cover and cook for 8 hours on low.
5. Divide into plates and serve.

19. Burger with Oaxaca, Avocado and Fresh Salsa:

Nutrition Value per serving:

Serves: 4
Calories: 341.1
Fat: 11.3 g
Protein: 15.8 g
Carbohydrates: 6 g

Ingredients:

- ½ lb. ground beef
- 1 teaspoon salt
- 1 teaspoon black pepper
- ½ teaspoon cayenne
- ½ teaspoon garlic powder
- 1 tablespoon jalapeno pepper, chopped
- 1 egg
- 1 tablespoon whole cream butter
- ½ cup Oaxaca cheese
- 1 avocado, sliced
- ½ cup tomato, diced
- ¼ cup red onion, diced
- ½ cup fresh cilantro, chopped
- Lettuce leaves for serving, optional

Directions:

1. Place the ground beef in a bowl and season with salt, black pepper, cayenne powder and garlic powder.
2. Add the jalapeno pepper and egg. Mix until the egg is incorporated through, taking care to not over handle the meat.
3. Loosely form the meat into burger. Place the butter in a skillet over medium heat.
4. Once the butter has melted place the burgers in the skillet and cook, occasionally spooning the butter over the burgers, until desired doneness is reached. Add the cheese and remove from heat.
5. While the burgers are cooking combine the tomatoes, onions and cilantro.
6. Set aside.
7. Place the burgers on serving plates or lettuce leaves, if using.
8. Top with avocado and fresh salsa before serving.

20. Tantalizing Pork Chops with Cumin Butter and Garlic:

Nutrition Value per serving:

Serves: 4
Calories: 364
Fat: 17 g
Protein: 51 g
Carbohydrates: 3 g

Ingredients:

- pounds of pork sirloin chops with the bone
- ½ cup of salsa
- 3 tablespoons of butter
- 5 tablespoons lime juice
- ½ teaspoon of ground cumin
- ¾ teaspoon of garlic powder
- ¾ teaspoon of salt
- ¾ teaspoon of black pepper

Directions:

1. Combine the spices and season the pork chops
2. Melt the butter in a saucepan and brown the brown the pork chops for 3 minutes on each side.
3. Place the chops into the slow cooker and pour the salsa over the top.
4. Cover and cook on high for 3-4 hours.
5. *Divide into plates and serve.*

21. Delightful Balsamic Oregano Chicken:

Nutrition Value per serving:

Serves: 4
Calories: 190
Fat: 6 g
Protein: 26 g
Carbohydrates: 6 g

Ingredients:

- 6 pieces of boneless, skinless chicken
- 2 cans of diced tomatoes, 14.5 ounces
- 1 large onion, thinly sliced
- 4 cloves of garlic
- ½ cup of balsamic vinegar
- 1 tablespoon of olive oil
- 1 tablespoon of dried rosemary
- 1 teaspoon of dried basil
- ½ teaspoon of thyme
- Salt and pepper.

Directions:

1. In a small bowl combine all the ingredients except the chicken. Mix them together thoroughly.
2. Place the chicken in the slow cooker and pour the remaining ingredients over the top.
3. Cover and cook on high for 4 hours.

22. Smoked Whitefish Salad:

Nutrition Value per serving:

Serves: 4
Calories: 386.7
Fat: 12.2 g
Protein: 31 g
Carbohydrates: 4.2 g

Ingredients:

- 1 lb. smoked whitefish, chunked
- ½ cup celery, diced
- ½ cup red onion, diced
- ½ cup crème, fraise
- ½ cup cream cheese
- 1 tablespoon fresh chives
- 1 tablespoon fresh dill
- 2 teaspoons lemon juice

Directions:

1. Place the whitefish in a bowl with the celery and red onion. Toss to mix. If you would like a less chunky salad, you can place the ingredients in a food processor and pulse until broken down into smaller pieces.
2. In another bowl combine the crème fraise, cream cheese, chives, dill and lemon juice, Add salt and pepper to taste if desired.
3. Blend until creamy.
4. Add the cream mixture to the whitefish and mix until blended.
5. Cover and refrigerate for two hours before serving.

23. Beautiful BBQ Ribs:

Serves: 4

Nutrition Value per serving:

Calories: 420
Fat: 28 g
Protein: 38 g
Carbohydrates: 14 g

Ingredients:

- 3 pounds of pork ribs
- 1 tablespoon of olive oil
- 1 can of tomato paste, 28 ounces
- ½ can of hot water
- ½ cup of vinegar
- 6 tablespoons of Worcestershire sauce
- 4 tablespoon of dry mustard
- 1 tablespoon of chili powder
- 1 teaspoon of ground cumin
- 1 teaspoon of powdered sweetener of your choice
- Salt and pepper

Directions:

1. Heat the olive oil in a large frying pan and brown the ribs.
2. Place them in the crock pot
3. In a small bowl, combine the remainder of the ingredients, whisk together thoroughly and pour over the ribs.

4. Cook for 8 hours on low.

24. Spicy Tuna Salad over Arugula and Spinach with Red Onion:

Nutrition Value per serving:

Serves: 4
Calories: 269.9
Fat: 12.1 g
Protein: 35.2 g
Carbohydrates: 4.4 g

Ingredients:

- 1 lb. grilled tuna steak, chunked
- ¼ cup olive oil
- ¼ cup rice vinegar
- 1 tablespoon sriracha or cayenne sauce adjust amount to suit personal taste
- 2 cups arugula, torn
- 3 cups fresh spinach, torn
- 1 cup red onion, sliced

Directions:

1. In a bowl combine the olive oil, rice vinegar and sriracha or cayenne sauce.
2. Whisk until well blended.

3. Place the tuna in a bowl and pour the dressing in the tuna. Cover and refrigerate for two hours.
5. Combine the arugula, spinach and onion. Toss to mix.
6. Place the salad mixture in a large bowl or individual serving plates.
7. Top with the marinated grilled tuna, using the extra marinade as dressing if desired.

25. Chicken salad:

Serves: 6

Nutrition Value per serving:

Calories: 279
Fat: 19 g
Net carb: 0 g
Fiber: 25 g
Protein: 25 g

Ingredients:

- chicken breast lbs
- 3 celery stalks, diced
- ½ C Paleo Mayonnaise
- 2 tea spoon Brown mustard
- ½ tea spoon salt
- 2 table spoon Dill, fresh, chopped
- ¼ C Pecans, chopped

Directions:

1. On a baking sheet, line the bottom with parchment paper. Preheat the oven to 45^0 degrees Fahrenheit.
2. Bake the chicken for about 15 minutes or until cooked through.
3. While the chicken is baking, in a bowl, combine the celery, Mayonnaise, mustard, and salt. Place in the fridge to stay cool.
4. Remove the chicken from the oven when done cooking and chop into bite-sized chunks. Allow to

cool and then mix into the bowl with the other ingredients.

5. It is best to allow this to cool overnight in the fridge; however, it can be eaten immediately. Prior to serving, top with chopped dill and pecans.

26. Simple Taco Salad

Serves 6

Ingredients:

- 32 ounces of Ground Pork
- 9 ounces of Shredded Cheddar Cheese
- 6 teaspoons of McCormick Taco Seasoning
- 12 tablespoons of Salsa
- 12 tablespoons of Sour Cream
- Cayenne Pepper
- 6 Romaine Leafs

Directions:

1. Brown your pork in skillet.
2. Add spices and taco seasoning once meat is browned.
3. Cook until taco seasoning is incorporated.
4. Allow to cool and evenly divide into 6 containers.
5. Add cheese to each of the containers.
6. Add Romaine to containers.
7. Add salsa and sour cream to your bowl.
8. Serve and Enjoy!

Nutritional Value - Serving Size 1/6:

38 g of Protein.

51 g of Fat.

5 g of Carbs.

647 Calories.

27. Grilled Halloumi Salad

Serves 1

Ingredients:

- 1 Persian Cucumber
- 3 ounces of Halloumi Cheese
- 5 Grape Tomatoes
- 1/2 ounce of Chopped Walnuts
- 1 handful of Baby Arugula
- Balsamic Vinegar
- Olive Oil
- Salt

Directions:

1. Cut your halloumi cheese into approximately 1/3 inch sized slices.
2. Grill these slices for 3 to 5 minutes on both sides. Should have nice grill marks on both sides.
3. Prep your salad by washing then cutting your vegetables. Tomatoes in half and cucumbers into smaller slices. Chop your walnuts and add them in your salad bowl.
4. Wash baby arugula and add to your bowl.
5. Arrange grilled halloumi cheese on top of salad. Add some salt. Dress salad with balsamic vinegar and olive oil.
6. Serve and Enjoy!

Nutrition Value per serving:

21 g of Protein.

47 g of Fat.

7 g of Carbs.

560 Calories.

28. Berry & Chicken Summer Salad

Serves 2

Ingredients:

- 1 Chicken Breast
- 6 Diced Strawberries
- 2 cups of Spinach
- 3/4 cup of Blueberries
- 3 tablespoons of Crumbled Feta Cheese
- 3 tablespoons of Raspberry Balsamic Vinegar
- 1/2 cup of Chopped Walnuts

Directions:

1. Cut chicken breast up into small cubes and cook in your pan. When done place on your plate to cool off.
2. Gather your other ingredients and add them to a big bowl. Add your dressing.
3. Add your chicken and toss the salad.
4. Serve and Enjoy!

Nutrition Value per serving:

21 g of Protein.
19 g of Fat.
16 g of Carbs.
335 Calories.

29. Simple Chicken Salad

Serves 6

Ingredients:

- 4 Chicken Breasts
- 105 g of Green Peppers
- 125 g of Celery
- 20 g of Green Onions
- 3/4 Cup of Mayo
- 3/4 Cup of Sugar-Free Sweet Relish
- 3 Large Hardboiled Eggs

Directions:

1. Preheat your oven to 350 degrees.
2. Add your chicken to your oven safe pan.
3. Cook for approximately 45 to 60 minutes until your chicken is finished cooking.
4. Place 3 eggs in your pan and cover them with water. Bring it to a boil and then cook approximately 15 minutes once water is boiling.
5. While chicken is in oven cooking, chop up your onions, celery, and peppers.
6. Once your chicken is out of your oven let it cool down and then chop up.
7. Combine all ingredients in a large bowl.
8. Chop up your eggs and mix in. Add eggs last.
9. Split into 6 separate portions or containers.
10. Serve and Enjoy!

Nutritional Value - Serving Size 1/6:

43 g of Protein.

25 g of Fat.

2 g of Carbs.

413 Calories.

30. Easy Buffalo Wings

Serves 2

Ingredients:

- 6 Chicken Wings 6 Drumettes & 6 Wingettes
- 2 tablespoons of Butter
- 1/2 cup of Frank's Red Hot Sauce
- Paprika
- Garlic Powder
- Pepper
- Salt
- Cayenne optional

Directions:

1. Break each chicken wing into 2 different pieces. The drumettes and wingettes, getting rid of the tips.
2. Pour hot sauce over your wings. Enough to lightly coat them.
3. Season wings with spices and cover them. Place in refrigerator for 1 hour.
4. Place broiler on high and put your oven rack 6 inches from broiler. Put your aluminum paper on a baking sheet. Place wings on your sheet with enough room so the flames can reach their sides.
5. Cook for 8 minutes under your broiler. Wings should turn dark brown on top. May turn black if very close to the flame.

6. Melt your butter on the oven top and add rest of hot sauce. Can also add cayenne if you want wings to be spicier.
7. Once butter has melted take off heat.
8. Take wings from broiler and flip them. Cook another 6 to 8 minutes.
9. Once good and browned on all sides take out of your broiler and add to bowl.
10. Pour butter-hot sauce mixture over wings. Toss wings to coat evenly.
11. Serve and Enjoy!

Nutritional Value - Serving Size 6 Wings:

48 g of Protein.

46 g of Fat.

1 gram of Carbs:

620 Calories.

31. Oopsie Rolls

Serves 12

Ingredients:

- 3 Large Eggs
- 1/8 teaspoon of Cream of Tartar
- 3 ounces of Cream Cheese
- 1/8 teaspoon of Salt

Directions:

1. Preheat your oven to 300 degrees.
2. Separate eggs from egg yolks. Place each in different bowls.
3. With an electric hand mixer beat your egg whites until they get very bubbly.
4. Add in your cream of tarter. Beat it until a stiff peak is formed.
5. In egg yolk bowl, add your 3 ounces of cream cheese and salt.
5. Beat egg yolk mixture until your yolks are a pale looking yellow and they have doubled in their size.
6. Fold the egg whites into the egg yolk mixture. Don't use an electric hand mixer. Gently fold it together.
7. Line a cookie sheet with parchment paper and spray with some oil or grease. Dollop your batter as big as you want them. I make 12 of equal size and the nutritional value amount reflects that.
8. Bake approximately 30 to 40 minutes. They are

done when the tops of oopsie rolls are firm and golden.

9. Let cool on wire rack.
10. Serve and Enjoy!

Nutritional Value - Serving Size 1 Roll:

2.3 g of Protein

3.8 g of Fat.

0 g of Carbs.

45 Calories

32. Cucumber Sushi Rolls

Serves 2

Ingredients:

- 1/2 pound of Tuna Steak
- 2 Cucumbers
- 1/2 of an Avocado
- 8 Shrimp
- 2 tablespoons of Mayonnaise
- 2 teaspoons of Sriracha
- 1/2 teaspoon of Sesame Seeds
- 1 stalk of Green Onion

Directions:

1. Peel your cucumbers and cut off their ends. You want to have two 6 to 8 inch long cylindrical shaped cucumbers when done.
2. Use a wet long knife and lay the edge of it against an edge of your cucumber. Begin cutting into it. Knife should be barely visible under your transparent cucumber.
3. Once cucumber is cut to its seeds gather your other ingredients.
4. Mix mayo and sriracha to make spicy mayo.
5. You're now ready to begin rolling! Take the end of your cucumber with your fish and begin rolling it onto itself. Make sure to keep your roll tight so that no air pockets form. The ingredients need to

stick to one another, otherwise, they'll fall right out.

6. Once you're almost done rolling it and only have approximately 2 to 3 inches left of your cucumber, spread some of your spicy mayo on your cucumber and finish the roll. The mayonnaise will act as sort of glue to help keep your cucumber sealed.
7. Next, carefully slice your cucumber into 1/2 inch to 1-inch rounds. Hold both sides of your cucumber as slicing to help maintain its shape.
8. You should now have 6 to 8 pieces of sushi per roll. Chop up green onion and sprinkle on top.
9. Serve and Enjoy!

Nutrition Value per serving:

36 g of Protein.

17 g of Fat.

2.5 g of Carbs.

322 Calories.

Dinner

33. Stuffed Chicken Breast cream cheese, thyme, basil, garlic and smoked ham:

Serves: 4

Nutrition Value per serving

Calories: 427.5
Fat: 13.6 g
Protein: 36.0 g
Carbohydrates: 3.5 g

Ingredients:

- 1 lb. chicken breasts
- 1 teaspoon salt
- 1 teaspoon black pepper
- 1 cup cream cheese
- 1 tablespoon fresh thyme
- ¼ cup fresh basil
- 2 cloves garlic, crushed and minced
- 1 cup smoked ham, diced
- 1 tablespoon olive oil

Directions:

1. Preheat the oven to 350 F. and line a baking pan with aluminum foil.
2. Take each chicken breast and slice along one side,

about two thirds of the way in to create a space to stuff the chicken.

3. Season the chicken with salt and black pepper.
4. In a bowl combine the cream cheese, thyme, basil, garlic and ham. Mix until well blended.
5. Place equal amounts of the stuffing mixture into the center of each piece of chicken. Secure with cooking twine, if necessary.
6. Heat the olive oil in a skillet over medium heat. Add the chicken and cook for 2-3 minutes per side, or until lightly browned. Transfer the chicken to the baking dish and place in the oven.
7. Cook for an additional 20 minutes or until the chicken is cooked through and no longer pink.

Enjoy the Dinner hot!

34. Walnut Salad Tossed with Goat Cheese and Bacon:

Serves: 4
Nutrition Value per serving:

Calories: 259
Fat: 4.9 g
Protein: 5 g
Carbohydrates: 3.5 g

Ingredients:

- 6 cups dark salad greens
- ¼ cup walnut oil
- 1 tablespoon warm bacon grease
- ¼ cup apple cider vinegar
- 1 tablespoon fresh tarragon
- ½ teaspoon salt
- ½ teaspoon black pepper
- ¼ cup walnuts, chopped
- ¼ cup bacon, chopped
- ¼ cup goat cheese
- 1 tablespoon pomegranate seeds

Directions:

1. In a bowl combine the walnut oil, bacon grease, apple cider vinegar, tarragon, salt and black pepper. Whish until well blended.
2. Add the salad greens to large bowl and drizzle the dressing over them.

3. Toss to coat.
4. Next, add in the walnuts, bacon, Goat cheese and pomegranate seeds. Toss to mix and serve.

Enjoy the Dinner hot!

35. Easy Meatball Crock pot:

Serves: 4
Nutrition Value per serving:

Calories: 413
Fat: 17.4 g
Protein: 46.7 g
Carbohydrates: 2.5 g

Ingredients:

- 1 heaping tablespoon tomato paste
- 1 cup bone broth
- Sea salt and pepper
- ½ teaspoon cumin
- 1 lb. ground beef
- Small handful fresh parsley, diced
- Sea salt
- 2 tablespoons butter or ghee
- ½ large head a cauliflower

Directions:

1. Put the meat in a bowl along with pepper, salt, paprika and cumin. Mix well to blend.
2. Make the meat into one-inch meatballs and put the balls at the bottom of a Crockpot.
3. Then mix the paste and the broth in a bowl and pour over the meatballs. Set the Crockpot on high and cook for about 2 hours.
4. Once the meatballs are cooked through, chop the cauliflower into florets and then steam them until well

cooked.

5. Now discard the water and in salt, butter and pepper. Blend the mixture using an immersion blender until smooth.
6. Put the cauliflower mash into serving plate, top with meatballs and enough amount of sauce on top.
7. Garnish with parsley and enjoy.

Enjoy the Dinner hot!

36. Chocolate Chicken Mole:

Serves: 3
Nutrition Value per serving:

Calories: 402.1
Fat: 20.4 g
Protein: 37 g
Carbohydrates: 20.6g

Ingredients:

- ¼ teaspoon chili powder
- ¼ teaspoon cinnamon power, ground
- ½ teaspoon cumin powder
- ½ teaspoon sea salt
- 25 oz. 35.4 g dark chocolate 70% or above
- 2 tablespoons creamy almond butter
- 2 ½ dried New Mexico chili peppers rehydrated and chopped
- 3-4 whole tomatoes peeled, seeded and chopped
- 2 cloves garlic crushed or minced
- ½ medium onion chopped
- 1 tablespoon ghee
- Sea salt

Directions:

1. 1 lb. chicken pieces bone in breasts and legs, without skin cilantro avocado and jalapeno, chopped
2. Season the chicken with salt and pepper and set aside. Put a pan over medium heat on a skillet then add in ghee.

3. Once melted, add in chicken add brown it on both sides. If the chicken is large, you can do it in batches.
4. Now transfer the chicken to a Crockpot. Then add in onion to the pan with chicken then sauté until golden. Add in garlic and sauté for about a minute or so.
5. Once done, move the garlic and onion to the Crockpot along with spices, salt, dark chocolate, almond butter, chili peppers and tomatoes.
6. Cook until the chicken is tender and can easily pull about, or for about 6-8 hours.
7. To serve, top with jalapeno, cilantro and avocado.

Enjoy the Dinner hot!

37. Homemade Pork Verde:

Serves: 10
Nutrition Value per serving:

Calories: 192
Fat: 8 g
Protein: 24 g
Net carbo: 1.5 g

Ingredients:

- 3 lbs. of Tomatillos
- 1 pc. Garlic, minced
- 2 lbs. of pork Chops, diced
- 1 large onion, sliced
- 1 large jalapeno

Directions:

1. Start the preparation by cutting onions into quarters and the jalapenos in half. Skin the tomatoes and also cut it in half.
2. Roast the tomatoes in the oven. To roast your veggies, set your oven on broil and place the tomatoes in the oven until their tops turned semi-black. Once done, take it out of the oven and blend using a blender till it turns into a sauce like mixture.
3. Place the sauce and diced pork into the instant pot and set to manual cooking for 6 minutes. When the pressure cooker beeps, naturally release the pressure for about 10 minutes. Open the valve and release the remaining steam.
4. Serve with a bowl

Enjoy the Dinner hot!

38. Sriracha Lime Flank Steak:

Serves: 2
Nutrition Value per serving:

Calories: 504
Fat: 32 g
Protein: 48 g
Net carbo: 5.5 g
Ingredients:

- 16 OZ Flank Steak
- Slat
- Pepper
- Sriracha Lime Sauce
- 1 lime
- 2 tablespoon Sriracha
- 2 tablespoon olive oil
- 1 teaspoon

Directions:

1. Liberally season the steak with salt and pepper. Broil for 5 minutes on each side for medium-rare. Add 1 minute on each side for medium and 2 minutes for well-done.
2. Cover the steak and let rest for 5 minutes. Meanwhile, squeeze fresh lime in a bowl and mix with sriracha, vinegar, salt and pepper. While whisking these together, slowly pour in olive oil to create an emulsion and thicken the sauce.
3. Slice steak thin and serve with sauce and your choice of side, like roasted asparagus.

Enjoy the Dinner hot!

39. Butter Chicken:

Serves: 6
Nutrition Value per serving:

Net carbo : 5.5 g
Fat: 19.4 g
Protein: 37 g
Carbohydrates: 20.6g

Ingredients:

- 4 tablespoons unsalted butter
- 2 onions, diced
- 2 pounds boneless, skinless chicken breasts
- A 2 inch piece of ginger, cut into 1/2-inch pieces
- 4 garlic cloves
- ½ cup sliced almonds
- 1 cup plain yogurt
- 2 teaspoons graham spice
- 1 teaspoon salt
- 1 can diced tomatoes, drained
- ¼ cup heavy cream

How to make it

1. Cut the chicken breasts into 1-inch pieces.
2. In a small pot, melt the butter over a medium flame and then add the onions. Boil the onion for 4-5 minutes.
3. In a food processor, combine the ginger, the garlic, the almonds, the yogurt, the graham spice, and the salt. Blend it until the mixture become smooth.

4. And the tomatoes to the food processor and pulse once or twice to combine it with the mix.
5. Put the chicken at the bottom of the slow cooker, and pour the tomato mix over to of it.
6. Cook on low for 4-5 hours.
7. Serve over rice

Enjoy the Dinner hot!

40. Chicken Hearts Stroganoff:

Nutrition Value per serving:

Serves: 3
Calories: 249.9
Fat: 3 g
Protein: 38.7 g
Net carbs: 9.7 g

Ingredients:

- 7 tablespoons full fat Greek yogurt
- 2 tablespoons heavy cream or coconut milk
- ½ cup chicken stock
- ¼ tablespoon cayenne pepper
- ¼ tablespoon paprika
- ½ teaspoon salt
- ½ tablespoon Dijon mustard
- 2 cloves garlic, minced
- 1 lb. chicken hearts, cut into thirds
- ½ lb. 8 ouncewhole mushrooms, sliced
- ½ onion, thinly sliced

Directions:

1. Add mushrooms and onions to the slow cooker then top with chicken hearts. The meat should not touch the sides.
2. Add in species, garlic and mustard then pour in chicken stock.
3. Cover the Crockpot and cook for 6 hours on low heat. Then turn off the heat, let cool for 5 minutes and then stir in yoghurt and cream.
4. Let cool for about 5 minutes before serving. If need be, you can use other types of thickeners such as sour cream or Crème fraiche. Serve with steamed veggies.

Enjoy the Dinner hot!

41. Rosemary Oven-Fried Chicken:

Nutrition Value per serving:

Serves: 2
Calories: 248
Fat: 8.7 g
Protein: 27.4 g
Net carbo: 15.1 g

Ingredients:

- 1/8 cup buttermilk
- 1 tablespoon Dijon Mustard
- 2 4-ounceChicken Breast
- 1/6 cup whole-wheat panko
- 1/6 cup finely chopped dry-roasted cashews
- 3/8 teaspoon minced fresh rosemary
- 1/8 teaspoon kosher slat
- 1/8 teaspoon freshly ground black pepper
- 1/8 teaspoon ground red pepper
- Butter cooking spray
- 2 teaspoon honey

Directions:

1. Preheat oven to 425 degrees.
2. Combine buttermilk and mustard in a small dish, stir well. Add chicken to mixture to coat.
3. Heat a small saucepan over medium heat; cook the chicken for 3 minutes or until they are browned. Combine cashews, and the remaining ingredients together in a bowl, coat chicken with buttermilk

mixture.

4. Put the panko in a shallow dish; coat the chicken well with whole wheat panko.
5. Place chicken in a baking pan cover with aluminum foil. Back the chicken at 425 F for 25 minutes or until ready.
6. Spread chicken with honey.
7. Serve and enjoy!

Enjoy the Dinner hot!

42. Low Carb Chicken Parmesan:

Nutrition Value per serving:

Serves: 2
Calories: 600
Fat: 32 g
Protein: 74 g
Net carbo: 3 g

Ingredients:

- 1 OZ pork rinds
- 2 tablespoon parmesan cheese
- 1 egg
- 1 lb chicken breast
- 1/ 2 cup marinara sauce
- 1/ 2 cup shredded mozzarella
- Salt
- Pepper
- Oregano
- Garlic powder

Directions:

1. Preheat oven to 350 F.
2. Crush up pork rinds and Parmesan cheese in a food processor or Magic bullet. Pour out your "Breading" into a shallow dish for later. Don't blend for too long, the mixture will become wet, you want it coarsely crumbed/ground.
3. Lay some cling wrap over the chicken breasts to avoid splatterand pound them until they are an even 1/2 inch.
4. This is to ensure the chicken is cooked evenly, without the edges being too dry and the middles being under cooked
5. Beat an egg in a bowl and set it next to the "Breading". Submerge one chicken breast at a time into the egg wash.
6. Then press it firmly onto the breading dish, covering all sides well.
7. Place the chicken breasts onto an oiled baking sheet and season the tops with salt, pepper, oregano and garlic powder.
8. Bake in the oven for about 25 minutes. You should see a golden brown crust forming.
9. Take the chicken breasts out of the oven and pour marinara sauce over each one.
10. Top with a sprinkling of mozzarella cheese and place back in the oven for 15 more minutes so that the chicken finishes cooking and the cheese melts nicely.
11. Once times up, serve immediately with some spaghetti squash, zoodles or a bed of spinach.

Enjoy the Dinner hot!

43. Mexican Chicken Pollo Con Salsa Rojo:

Nutrition Value per serving:

Serves: 3
Calories: 250
Fat: 5 g
Protein: 15 g

Ingredients:

- 2 lbs. boneless, skinless chicken thighs cut into bite sizes
- 2 ounces pickled/canned jalapenos
- 1 small onion, chopped
- 3 cloves ground garlic
- 1 and ½ teaspoon ground cumin
- Chili powder and salt optional

Directions:

1. Set the instant pot to "sauté" cooking mode.
2. As the instant pot is heating, coat the chicken thighs with cumin, 1 teaspoon chili powder and salt.
3. Pour 2 teaspoon of oil into the instant pot once it's hot and add the pieces of coated chicken and let it cook for 4-5 minutes. This will help the chicken bloom to their full flavor.
4. Add all the other ingredients to the chicken in the instant pot and cover.
5. Cook at high pressure setting and allow it to cook for

15 minutes then allow for natural pressure release for 10 minutes. Release the remaining pressure.

6. Serve as tacos by shredding the chicken pieces a bit more using a fork.

Enjoy the Dinner hot!

44. Lemon Garlic Chicken in Slow cooker:

Nutrition Value per serving:

Serves: 2
Calories: 274
Fat: 16.7 g
Protein: 26.9g
Net carbo: 3.4 g

Ingredients:

- 1 pound of chicken breast
- 3/8 cup chicken broth
- 1-1/2 tablespoons lemon juice
- 1/ 2 lemon, sliced
- 1 tablespoon garlic, minced
- 1/2 teaspoon basil
- 1/4 teaspoon salt
- 1/8 teaspoon pepper
- 1/4 teaspoon garlic powder
- 1/4 teaspoon oregano
- 4 tablespoon melted butter

Directions:

1. In a medium bowl, mix all the spices and melted butter together. Rub the butter seasoning on both sides of chicken breast.
2. Heat a medium pan with butter; cook the seasoned chicken for 7-10 minutes for each side.
3. Place chicken breast in a slow cooker. Top the chicken breast with lemon slices.
4. Pour chicken broth in the slow cooker.
5. Cover and cook for 6-7 hours or for 3-4 hours on high.

Enjoy the Dinner hot!

45. Beef Chuck Pot Roast:

Nutrition Value per serving:

Serves: 2-3
Calories: 280
Fat: 13.2g
Protein: 35.5 g
Net carbo: 2.5 g

Ingredients:

- 1/4 can cream of celery soup or cream of mushroom soup
- 1/4 packet onion soup dry mix
- 1 lb beef for roasting

Directions:

1. Begin by stabbing the meat in a few places using a fork or knife, and place in crock-pot with the side with the fatty side facing up.
2. Add the dry onion soup on top and on sides followed with the can of mushroom or celery soup over the roast.
3. Spread it on top a little and now cover the slow cooker and turn it on.
4. At this point, cook for 3 hours on high or 5 hours set on low heat setting.
5. If need be, set the slow cooker on low and allow the roast in-in the morning to prepare for an evening meal.

Enjoy the Dinner hot!

Smoothie

46. Choco-Cashew Orange Smoothie

Prep Time: 10 MIN
Serve: 1
Ingredients:

- 1 cup cashew milk
- 1 handful of arugula leaves
- 1 tbsp chocolate whey protein powder
- 1/8 tsp orange extract
- Ice cubes

Directions:

1. Place all ingredients in your blender and blend until well united and smooth.
2. Add extra ice and serve.

Nutrition Value per serving:
Calories 45
Total Fats 1.05g
Net Carbs: 7g
Protein 3g

47. Strawberry Majoram Smoothie

Prep Time: 10 MIN
Serve: 1

Ingredients:

- 1/4 cup fresh or frozen strawberries
- 2 fresh marjoram leaves
- 2 tbsp heavy cream
- 1 cup unsweetened coconut milk
- 1 tbsp sugar-free vanilla syrup
- 1/2 tsp pure vanilla extract
- Ice cubes

Directions:

1. Place all ingredients in your blender and mix until become smooth.
2. If you wish you can add the ice cubes.
3. Serve.

Nutrition Value per serving:

Calories 292
Total Fats 26.7g
Net Carbs: 6g
Protein 2.8g
Fiber: 0.76g

48. The Green Fuel

Prep Time: 10 MIN
Serve: 1

Ingredients:

- 1 cup almond milk, unsweetened
- 1 cup baby spinach
- ½ ripe avocados
- ½ tbsp stevia
- 1 cup ice

Directions:

1. Place all the ingredients into a blender and blend until smooth.
2. Serve and consume immediately.

Nutrition Value per serving:
Calories 382
Total Fats 38.5g
Net Carbs: 11.5g
Protein 4.1g
Fiber 6.3g

49. Beet Cucumber Smoothie

Prep Time: 10 MIN
Serve: 4

Ingredients:

- 1 cup spinach leaves
- 2 cups cucumber peeled, seeded and chopped
- 1/2 cup carrot chopped
- 1/2 cup fresh beetroot
- 3/4 cup heavy whippingcream
- 4 tsp sweetener of your choice optional
- Handful of ground almonds
- 1 cup ice cubes
- 1 cup water

Directions:

1. Place all ingredients in a blender.
2. Pulse until smooth.
3. Serve immediately.

Nutrition Value per serving:
Calories 137.91
Total Fats 12.99g
Net Carbs: 3.4g
Protein 1.66g
Fiber: 1.44g

50. Cilantro and Ginger Smoothie

Prep Time: 10 MIN
Serve: 3

Ingredients:

- 1/2 cup fresh cilantro chopped
- 2-inch ginger, fresh
- 1 cucumber
- 2 Tbsp chia seeds
- 1/2 cup spinach, fresh
- 1 Tbsp almond butter
- Handful of ground almond
- 1 lime or lemon
- 2 cups water

Directions:

1. Blend spinach, cucumber, and water until smooth.
2. Add the remaining fruits and blend again.

Nutrition Value per serving:
Calories 102.72
Total Fats 6.92g
Net Carbs: 13.96g
Protein 71g
Fiber 6.88g

51. Green Coconut Smoothie

Prep Time: 10 MIN
Serve: 2

Ingredients:

- 1 cup coconut milk
- 1 green apple, cored and chopped
- 1 cup spinach
- 1 cucumber
- 2 Tbsp shaved coconut
- 1/2 cup water
- Ice cubes if needed

Directions:

1. Put all ingredients and ice in a blender; pulse until smooth.
2. Serve immediately.

Nutrition Value per serving:
Calories 216.57
Total Fats 16.56g
Net Carbs: 8.79g
Protein 2.88g
Fiber: 4g

52. Green Devil Smoothie

Prep Time: 10 MIN
Serve: 2

Ingredients:

- 3 cup kale, fresh
- 1/2 cup coconut yogurt
- 1/2 cup broccoli, florets
- 2 celery stalk, chopped
- 2 cup water
- 1 Tbsp lemon juice
- Ice cubes if needed

Directions:

1. Blend all ingredients together until smooth and slightly frothy.

Nutrition Value per serving:
Calories 117.09
Total Fats 4.98g
Net Carbs: 1.89g
Protein 4.09g
Fiber 6.18g

53. Green Dream Keto Smoothie

Prep Time: 10 MIN
Serve: 4

Ingredients:

- 1 cup raw cucumber, peeled and sliced
- 4 cups water
- 1 cup romaine lettuce
- 1 cup Haas avocado
- 2 Tbsp fresh basil
- Sweetener of your choice optional
- Handful of walnuts
- 2 Tbsp fresh parsley
- 1 Tbsp fresh ginger grated
- Ice cubes optional

Directions:

1 In a blender, combine all of the ingredients and pulse until smooth.
2 Add ice if used. Serve cold.

Nutrition Value per serving:
Calories 50.62
Total Fats 3.89g
Net Carbs: 1.07g
Protein 1.1g
Fiber 2.44g

54. Almond Lover Smoothie

Serves: 1 – 16 oz.
Nutrition Value per serving: -0- g Net Carbs
12 g Proteins
23 g Fat
511 Cal.

Ingredients:

- Medium banana – 1
- Almond milk – 8 oz. – 1 cup
- Plain non-fat Greek yogurt – .33 cup
- Cooked oats – .33 cup
- Almond butter – 2 tbsp.
- Almonds – 5

Direction

1 Measure all of the fixings into the cup of your NutriBullet or favorite high-speed machine.
2 Pour the milk up to the max-fill line. Blend until it is smooth and creamy.

55. Blackberry Cheesecake Smoothie

Serves: 1
Nutrition Value per serving: 6.7 g Net Carbs
6.4 g Proteins
53 g Fat
515 Cal.

Ingredients:

- Extra-virgin coconut oil – 1 tbsp.
- Fresh/frozen blackberries – .5 cup
- Water – .5 cup
- Coconut milk/heavy whipping cream – .25 cup
- Full-fat cream cheese or creamed coconut milk – .25 cup
- Sugar-free vanilla extract – .5 tsp.
- Liquid stevia – if desired – 3-5 drops

Direction

1 Toss all of the fixings into your blender.
2 Next, pulse until the mixture until it is smooth and frothy.
3 Add a few ice cubes and enjoy it in a chilled glass.

56. Blueberry - Banana Bread Smoothie

Serves: 2
Nutrition Value per serving: 4.7 g Net Carbs
3.1 g Proteins
23.3 g Fat
270 Cal.

Ingredients:
- Chia seeds – 1 tbsp.
- Golden flaxseed meal – 3 tbsp.
- Vanilla unsweetened coconut milk – 2cups
- Blueberries – .25 cup
- Liquid stevia – 10 drops
- MCT oil – 2 tbsp.
- Xanthan gum – .25 tsp.
- Banana extract – 1.5 tsp.
- Ice cubes – 2-3

Direction
1 Combine all of the ingredients into a blender.
2 Wait a few minutes for the seeds and flax to absorb some of the liquid.
3 Pulse for 1-2 minutes until well combined, and the texture you choose. Lastly, add the ice to your preference.

57. Blueberry & Kefir Smoothie

Serves: 2
Nutrition Value per serving: 6.6 g Net Carbs
3.9 g Proteins
50 g Fat
476 Cal.

Ingredients:

- Coconut milk kefir – 1.5 cups
- Fresh or frozen blueberries – .5 cup
- MCT oil – 2 tbsp.
- Water +ice cubes – .5 cup
- Sugar-free vanilla extract 1-2 tsp. or pure vanilla powder – .5 tsp.

Optional Ingredients:

- Collagen powder – 2 tbsp.
- Liquid stevia/your choice – 3-5 drops

Direction

1 Toss all of the ingredients into your blender
2 Pulse until the fixings are all mixed.
3 Serve in chilled glasses and enjoy your healthy choice!

58. Chocolate Smoothie

Serves: 1 large
Nutrition Value per serving: 4.4 g Net Carbs
34.5 g Proteins
46 g Fat
570 Cal.

Ingredients:

- Large eggs – 2
- Almond or coconut butter – 1-2 tbsp.
- Extra-virgin coconut oil – 1 tbsp.
- Coconut milk or heavy whipping cream – .25 cup
- Chia seeds – 1-2 tbsp.
- Cinnamon – .5 tsp.
- Plain or chocolate whey protein – .25 cup
- Stevia extract – 3-5 drops
- Unsweetened cacao powder – 1 tbsp.
- Water – .25 cup
- Ice – .5 cup
- Vanilla extract – .5 tsp.

Direction

1 Add the eggs along with the rest of fixings into the blender.
2 Pulse until frothy. Add to a chilled glass and enjoy.

59. Cinnamon Roll Smoothie

Serves: 1
Nutrition Value per serving: 0.6 g Net Carbs
26.5 g Proteins
3.25 g Fat
145 Cal.

Ingredients:

- Almond milk – 1 cup
- Vanilla protein powder – 2 tbsp.
- Vanilla extract – .25 tsp.
- Cinnamon – .5 tsp.
- Sweetener – 4 tsp.
- Flax meal – 1 tsp.
- Ice – 1 cup

Direction

1 Combine all of the fixings in a blender. Add the ice last.
2 Blend on the high setting for 30 seconds until thickened.

60. 5-Minute Mocha Smoothie

Serves: 3
Nutrition Value per serving: 4 g Net Carbs
3 g Proteins
16 g Fat
176 Cal.

Ingredients:

- Unsweetened almond milk – 1.5 cups
- Coconut milk – from the can – .5 cup
- Vanilla extract – 1 tsp.
- Instant coffee crystals – regular or decaffeinated – 1 tsp.
- Erythritol blend/granulated stevia- 3 tbsp.
- Unsweetened cocoa powder – 3 tbsp.
- Avocado – 1

Direction

1 Use a sharp knife to slice the avocado in half. Scoop the center out and discard the pit. Dice the avocado and add it along with the rest of the ingredients into the blender.
2 Mix well until smooth and serve.

61. Raspberry Avocado Smoothie

Serves: 2
Nutrition Value per serving: 4 g Net Carbs
2.5 g Proteins
20 g Fat
227 Cal.

Ingredients:

- Ripe avocado – 1
- Lemon juice – 3 tbsp.
- Water – 1.33 cups
- Frozen unsweetened raspberries/or choice of berries – .5 cup
- Your preference sugar equivalent – 1 tbsp. +1 t.

Direction

1 Blend all of the components in a blender until creamy smooth.
2 Empty the smoothie into two chilled glasses and enjoy!

Fat Bomb Recipes

62. Mocha Fat Bombs

Serves: 12

Nutritional values per serving:

Calories – 63, Fat – 6.8 g, Total Carbohydrate – 1.3 g, Net Carbohydrate – 0.3 g, Fiber – 1 g, Protein – 0.3 g

Ingredients

- 2 ½ tablespoons grass fed butter, unsalted, softened
- 1 shot espresso
- 1 tablespoon heavy whipping cream
- ½ scoop Perfect Keto MCT oil powder
- 1.5 ounces cream cheese, softened
- 2 tablespoons coconut oil
- 1 tablespoon monk fruit sweetener
- ¼ scoop Chocolate sea salt ketone supplement I used Perfect Keto brand

Direction

1. Add butter, espresso, cream cheese, cream and coconut oil into a heatproof bowl. Place the bowl in a double boiler. Stir frequently until it melts.
2. Remove the bowl from the double boiler and add rest of the ingredients. Stir and pour into 12 small silicone molds.
3. Place molds in the freezer until it sets. Remove from the molds and serve.
4. Place leftovers in an airtight container. Freeze

until use.

63. Peaches and Cream Fat Bombs

Serves: 12

Nutritional values per serving:

Calories – 43, Fat – 4.2 g, Total Carbohydrate – 1 g, Net Carbohydrate – 0.9 g, Fiber – 0.1 g, Protein – 0.5 g

Ingredients

- 2 tablespoons grass fed butter, unsalted, softened
- ½ cup frozen peaches, slightly warmed
- 3 ounces cream cheese, softened
- 1 ¾ tablespoons monk fruit sweetener
- 1/3 scoop Perfect Keto peaches and cream ketone supplement

Direction

1. Add butter, peaches, cream, 1-tablespoon monk fruit sweetener and peaches and cream ketone supplement into a mixing bowl.
2. Beat with a hand mixer until well incorporated.
3. Spoon the mixture into 12 small silicone molds. Sprinkle remaining monk fruit sweetener on top.
4. Place molds in the freezer until it sets. Remove from the molds and serve.

5. Place leftovers in an airtight container. Freeze until use.

64. Macadamia Chocolate Fat Bombs

Serves: 12

Nutritional values per serving:

Calories – 99, Fat – 16.9 g, Total Carbohydrate – 1.9 g, Net Carbohydrate – 0.9 g, Fiber – 1 g, Protein – 0.8 g

Ingredients

- 2 teaspoons vanilla extract
- A pinch salt
- 4 tablespoons swerve or erythritol
- 2/3 cup unrefined coconut oil
- 4 tablespoons cocoa powder, unsweetened
- 24 macadamia nuts

Direction

1. Add oil, swerve and vanilla into a bowl and whisk well.
2. Add cocoa powder and mix well.
3. Place 2 macadamia nuts in each of 12 small silicone molds. Divide the mixture into the molds. Sprinkle salt on top. Cool completely.
4. Refrigerate for a couple of hours until set.
5. Remove from the mold and serve. Place leftovers in an airtight container. Freeze until use.

65. Pumpkin Spice Fat Bombs

Serves: 12

Nutritional values per serving:

Calories – 78, Fat – 8.2 g, Total Carbohydrate – 3.1 g, Net Carbohydrate – 0.7 g, Fiber – 2.4 g, Protein – 0.7 g

Ingredients

- ¼ cup pecans
- 2 ounces cream cheese, softened
- ¼ cup coconut oil
- 2 tablespoons monk fruit sweetener
- ¼ cup pumpkin puree
- 1/8 teaspoon ground cinnamon
- 1 teaspoon pumpkin pie spice
- Avocado oil cooking spray

Direction

1. Place a small pan over medium heat. Spray with cooking spray.
2. Add pecans and sauté until toasted. Turn off the heat and transfer into a bowl.
3. Meanwhile, add coconut oil and cream cheese into the skillet. Place the skillet over low heat. Stir frequently until the mixture is well combined.
4. Transfer the mixture into a mixing bowl. Add pumpkin puree, pumpkin pie spice and monk

fruit sweetener and beat with an electric hand mixer until smooth and well combined.

5. Divide the mixture into 12 small silicone molds. Place pecans on top. Sprinkle cinnamon.
6. Place molds in the freezer until it sets. Remove from the molds and serve.
7. Place leftovers in an airtight container. Freeze until use.

66. Coffee Fat Bombs

Serves: 15

Nutrition Value per serving: -0- g Net Carbs
4 g Fat
-0- g Proteins
45 Cal.

Ingredients:

- Cream cheese – room temperature – 4.4 oz.
- Powdered Xylitol – 2 tbsp.
- Instant coffee – 1 tbsp.
- Coconut oil – 1 tbsp.
- Unsweetened cocoa powder – 1 tbsp.
- Room temperature butter – 1 tbsp.

Directions

1 Take the butter and cream cheese out of the fridge about an hour before it's time to begin.
2 With a blender/food processor, blitz the xylitol and coffee into a fine powder. Add the hot water to form a pasty mix.
3 Blend in the butter, cream cheese, cocoa powder, and coconut oil.
4 Add to ice cube trays and freeze a minimum of one to two hours.
5 Use Ziploc bags to keep them fresh in the freezer.

67. Coffee Fat Bombs

Serves: 15
Nutrition Value per serving: -0- g Net Carbs
-0- g Proteins
4 g Fat
45 Cal.

Ingredients:

- Cream cheese – room temperature – 4.4 oz.
- Powdered xylitol – 2 tbsp.
- Instant coffee – 1 tbsp.
- Room temperature butter – 1 tbsp.
- Coconut oil – 1 tbsp.
- Unsweetened cocoa powder – 1 tbsp.

Preparation Direction:

1 With a blender/food processor, blitz the xylitol and coffee into a fine powder. Add the hot water to form a pasty mix.
2 Blend in the butter, cream cheese, cocoa powder, and coconut oil.
3 Add to ice cube trays and freeze a minimum of one to two hours.
4 Use Ziploc bags to keep them fresh in the freezer.

68. Craving Buster Fat Bombs

Serves: 32

Nutrition Value per serving: 2.25 g Net Carbs
1.75 g Proteins
22.5 g Fat
122.5 Cal.

Ingredients:

- Organic cacao powder – 1 cup
- Melted organic coconut oil – 1 cup
- Almond butter – 1 cup
- Muffin tins – 32-count

Preparation Direction:

1 Melt the oil and whisk in with the almond butter and cacao.
2 Spoon 1/2 tablespoon of the product into the 32 small paper muffin cups.
3 Freeze or refrigerate until hard and store in the fridge.
4 Note: If you want just one bomb; melt the oil and just add 1/2 tablespoon of each ingredient to enjoy.

69. Dark Chocolate Fat Bombs

Serves: 12
Nutrition Value per serving: 5.6 g Net Carbs
10.5 g Fat
4 g Proteins
96 Cal.

Ingredients:

- Stevia extract – 1 tsp.
- Butter/coconut oil – .5 cup
- Almond butter – .5 cup
- Dark chocolate – 85% or higher – 3 oz.
- Sea salt – .25 tsp.

Preparation Direction:

1 With the use of a double boiler, combine all of the components in the recipe until smooth.
2 Empty the mixture into 12 ice trays and freeze for a minimum of one hour.
3 Serve or enjoy when the sugar urge strikes.

70. Dark Chocolate Raspberry Fat Bombs

Serves: 14
Nutrition Value per serving:
2.6 g Net Carbs
2.2 g Proteins
17 g Fat
164 Cal.

Ingredients:

- Extra-virgin coconut oil – 3 tbsp.
- Cocoa butter – .5 cup
- Unsweetened dark chocolate – 100% cacao – 4.2 oz.
- Unsweetened vanilla extract – 1 tsp. or 1 vanilla bean
- Unsweetened cacao powder – .33 cup
- Stevia extract – vanilla/clear/chocolate – 20-25 drops
- Swerve or Erythritol – powdered – 1/2 – 3/4 cup

Direction

1 Roast the almonds in a pan for five minutes.
2 Add an almond to each raspberry and freeze for one hour.
3 Using a dish over a pan of hot water or a double boiler, melt the unsweetened chocolate, coconut oil, and cocoa butter. Powder the Swerve for a smooth texture in a blender.
4 Remove the seeds from the bean if usingby slicing the bean lengthwise and scraping out the seeds. Add them along with the unsweetened cacao, stevia, and

powdered Erythritol.

5. Pour the mixture into papers with the use of a mini muffin tin, one tablespoon for each one. Add two loaded raspberries and pour one more tablespoon of the chocolate to cover.
6. Put the bombs in the freezer until set, for about 30 minutes.

Salads

71. Keto Caesar Salad

Calories per serving 468
Serves 4

Ingredients

- 300 g chicken breasts
- 90 g bacon
- 200 g Romaine lettuce
- 50 g grated parmesan cheese
- 1 tbsp olive oil
- ½ cup Homemade mayonnaise
- 1 tbsp Dijon mustard
- ½ lemon juice
- tbsp chopped anchovy filets
- 1 pressed garlic clove to taste
- salt and pepper

Keto Caesar Salad Cooking
<u>Salad</u>

1. Preheat the oven to 400 ºF. Grease baking sheet. Place the chicken breasts on sheet.
2. Drizzle olive oil on top of the chicken. Add salt and pepper to breasts.
3. Bake the chicken for 20 minutes, until fully cooked.
4. Fry the bacon until crispy in the frying pan.
5. Shred the lettuce and place on plate.
6. Place sliced chicken on plate, crumble bacon on top.
7. Season the salad with dressing and 30 g grated Parmesan.

Dressing

Mix anchovies' filets, homemade mayonnaise, Dijon mustard, lemon juice, 2 tbsp grated Parmesan cheese, garlic clove, salt and pepper with immersion blender. Chill in the refrigerator.

72. Greek Salad

Calories per serving 252
Serves 4
Ingredients

- ripe tomatoes
- ½ cucumber
- ½ red onion
- ½ green bell pepper
- 200 g feta cheese
- 10 lack olives
- tbsp olive oil
- ½ tbsp red wine vinegar
- tsp dried oregano
- salt and pepper

Directions:

Salad

1 Cut the tomatoes and cucumber into bite-sized pieces.
2 Thinly slice the bell pepper and onion.
3 Arrange the ingredients on a plate.
4 Add feta and olives.
5 Drizzle the salad with the dressing.
6 Sprinkle with oregano.

Dressing

Mix the olive oil and vinegar. Add salt and pepper to

taste.

73. Avocado and Chicken Salad with Bacon

Calories per serving 189
Serves 4

Ingredients

- 1 slice bacon
- ½ medium avocado
- 100 g chicken breast
- 30 g cheddar cheese
- 1 hard-boiled egg
- 200 g Romaine lettuce
- 1 tbsp olive oil
- 1 tbsp apple cider vinegar
- salt and pepper

Directions:

1. Chop the lettuce. Place into salad bowl.
2. Chop bacon, avocado, chicken breast, Cheddar cheese, and egg. Place the ingredients atop the lettuce.
3. Add oil and vinegar. Sprinkle salt and pepper.

74. Walnuts Fennel and Goat Cheese Green Bean Salad

Calories per serving 338-422
Serves 8-10

Ingredients

- 1 ½ tbsp Dijon mustard
- tbsp white wine vinegar
- ¾ tsp kosher salt
- ½ tsp freshly ground black pepper
- 1/3 cup extra-virgin olive oil
- 900 g trimmed green beans
- 1 small fennel bulb
- ¾ cup walnuts
- 400 g fresh Goat cheese

Directions:
Salad

1 Boil salted water in a large saucepan. Add the green beans. Cook for 6-8 minutes.
2 Drain and cool under cold water.
3 Slice the fennel bulb into half-moons.
4 Toast and coarsely chop walnuts.
5 Crumble the goat cheese.
6 Combine the green beans, fennel, and walnuts.

Before serving add the goat cheese.

7 Top with dressing.

Dressing

Whisk mustard, salt, vinegar, and pepper. Add the oil and combine.

75. Keto Cobb Salad

Calories per serving 190-381
Serves 2-4

Ingredients

- cherry tomatoes
- ½ avocado
- 1 hard-boiled egg
- cups mixed green salad
- 60 g cooked chicken breast
- 30 g feta cheese
- ¼ cup cooked bacon
- 1 tbsp olive oil
- ½ tbsp white wine vinegar
- Salt and pepper

Directions:

1 Cut the tomatoes, egg, and avocadoes into slices.
2 Shred cooked chicken breast.
3 Crumble feta cheese.
4 Place the mixed green salad into salad bowl or on a plate.
5 Place tomatoes, avocado, egg, bacon, cheese, and chicken on top of the salad.
6 Dress the salad with olive oil and white wine vinegar. Salt and pepper to taste. You can use one tbsp Ranch dressing.

76. Keto Chicken Salad

Calories per serving 627
Serves 2

Ingredients

- 285 g chicken breast
- 90 g thin-cut bacon slices
- 200 g avocado
- 12- g mixed leaf greens
- 60 ml Paleo Ranch Dressing
- Duck fat for greasing

Keto Chicken Salad Directions:

1 Preheat the oven to 400 °F.
2 Crisp the chicken breasts. Season with salt and pepper.
3 Grease pan with fat. Place breasts skin side down on the pan. Fry for 5-6 minutes. Flip the chicken and cook 30 seconds. Than transfer pan in the oven. Cook 10-15 minutes, until chicken is cooked through.
4 Place the slices bacon on the bake sheet. Bake the bacon slices in the oven until crispy. Alternatively, crisp the bacon in a frying pan.
5 Remove chicken from the oven. Cool for 5 minutes.
6 Slice the avocado and cooked chicken.
7 Place leafy greens on the plate. Add avocado, crispy bacon and sliced chicken.
8 Top with Ranch dressing.

Sauces And Dressing

77. Cheese Paste with Avocado

Calories per serving 854
Serves 4

Ingredients

- avocados
- 250 g Monterey Jack cheese
- 450 g cream cheese
- ½ tbsp minced garlic
- 1 tsp onion powder
- 1 tbsp pork rinds

Directions:

1. Peel the avocados, remove seeds.
2. Shred cheese and put in food processor. Add cream cheese. Mix well.
3. Add minced garlic and onion powder to cheese mixture, and mix again. Finish with pork rinds.

78. Creamy Guacamole

Calories per serving 277
Serves 4

Ingredients

- avocados
- ¾ cup chopped tomatoes
- 1/8 cup chopped onion
- 1 tsp salt
- ½ tsp chili powder
- ¼ tsp garlic powder
- one lime
- ¼ cup homemade mayonnaise

Directions:

Peel, slice, and smash avocado with a fork.

1 Add onion, tomatoes, lime juice, and chili powder. Mix well.
2 Top the guacamole with mayonnaise to keep from browning. Place dish in the refrigerator.

79. Homemade Mayonnaise

Calories per serving 111
Serves 4

Ingredients

- eggs
- 1 tbsp white vinegar
- 1 tsp sea salt
- 1 tsp dry mustard
- ¼ tsp Cayenne pepper
- 1 packet SweetLeaf Stevia
- ½ cups lite olive oil and avocado oil

Directions:

1. Mix eggs, white vinegar, sea salt, dry mustard, Cayenne pepper, and SweetLeaf Stevia in food processor or stand mixer.
2. Add the oil very slowly and continue to mix until the mixture begins to emulsify.

80. Ranch Dressing

Calories per serving 150
Serves 4
Ingredients

- ½ cup homemade mayonnaise
- 1 peeled clove garlic
- ½ cup well-shaken buttermilk
- 1 tbsp finely chopped onion
- tbsp finely chopped fresh chives
- 1/8 tsp sea salt
- ½ tsp dry mustard
- 1 tbsp finely chopped fresh flat-leaf parsley
- 1 tbsp finely chopped fresh dill
- ¼ tsp freshly ground black pepper

Directions:

3 Whisk the mayonnaise and buttermilk in a small bowl.
4 With a mortar and pestle, mash garlic, onion, and sea salt into a paste.
5 Add garlic-onion mixture and mustard to the buttermilk mixture. Whisk well.
6 Add the chives, dill, parsley, and black pepper. Mix the ingredients.
7 Season dressing with salt.

81. Low-Carb Lime Salad Dressing

Calories per serving 201
Serves 4
Ingredients

- Pinch salt
- Juice of one lime
- 1 clove garlic
- ½ jalapeno pepper
- ½ cup packed fresh cilantro
- 1/3 cup hemp oil

Directions:

Blend all the ingredients until smooth.

Dessert

82. Chocolate Mousse

Serves: 2
Nutrition Value per serving: 4 g Net Carbs
4 g Proteins
50 g Fat
460 Cal.

Ingredients:

- Heavy whipping cream – 1.5 tbsp.
- Swerve or another natural sweetener – 1 tbsp.
- Unsweetened cocoa powder – 1 tbsp.
- Butter – 4 tbsp.
- Cream Cheese – 4 tbsp.

Direction

1. Take the cream cheese and butter out of the refrigerator to become room temperature. Chill a bowl and whisk the cream. Store in the fridge.
2. In another dish, use a hand mixer to combine the sweetener, cream cheese, cocoa powder, and butter until well mixed.
3. Take out the refrigerated cream and fold into the chocolate mixture using a rubber scraper.
4. Portion into two dessert dishes and chill for one hour.

83. Cinnamon Roll Mousse

Serves: 4
Nutrition Value per serving: 5.1 g Net Carbs
29.3 g Fat
4.6 g Proteins
291 Cal.

Ingredients:

- Heavy whipping cream – .5 cup
- Softened full-fat cream cheese – 4.2 oz.
- Powdered Swerve or Erythritol – .25 cup
- Unsalted cashew butter or almond butter – 2 tbsp.
- Cinnamon – 1 tsp.
- Sugar-free vanilla extract – .5 tsp

Ingredients for the Drizzle:

- Coconut butter – 2 tbsp.
- Swerve or Erythritol – 1 tbsp.
- Virgin coconut oil – 1 tsp.
- Also Needed: 4 mason jars

Direction

1 Combine the heavy cream and cream cheese until smooth. Toss in the rest of the fixings sweetener to taste.
2 In another container, combine the drizzle components and place in the microwave. Using 10-second intervals, warm it up until it is syrupy.
3 Portion the mouse in the jars and drizzle with the syrup. Dust with some cinnamon and enjoy! It's good for up to five days in the fridge.

84. Keto Chia Pudding

Serves: 4
Nutrition Value per serving: 12 g Net Carbs
5 g Proteins
24 g Fat
273 Cal.

Ingredients:

- Whole ripe avocado – 1
- Chia seeds – .25 cup
- Medium dates – 2
- Almond or coconut milk – 1 cup
- Vanilla extract – .5 tsp.

Direction

1 Pour the milk, vanilla, avocado, and dates into a blender.
2 Blend until well mixed. Empty over the chia seeds and cover overnight in the refrigerator when you go to bed. You can also let it rest for two to four hours before serving.

85. Lemon Custard – Slow Cooker

Serves: 4
Nutrition Value per serving: 3 g Net Carbs
7 g Proteins
30 g Fat
319 Cal.

Ingredients:

- Fresh lemon juice – .25 cup
- Large egg yolks – 5
- Lemon zest – 1 tbsp.
- Liquid stevia – .5 tsp.
- Vanilla extract – 1 tsp.
- Coconut cream/whipping cream – 2 cups
- Optional: Whipped coconut cream
- Also Needed: Ramekins/4 small jars

Direction

1. Whisk the liquid stevia, egg yolks, lemon juice, lemon zest, and vanilla. Whip in the heavy cream. Divide into the four jars.
2. Add a rack in the cooker and arrange the jars on top of it. Add water to fill half of the way up the sides of the ramekins.
3. Secure the lid and cook three hours on low.
4. Transfer the jars from the cooker and cool to room temperature. Chill in the fridge approximately three hours.
5. Serve with the whipped cream if desired.

86. Pumpkin Custard - Crockpot

Serves: 6
Nutrition Value per serving: 3 g Net Carbs
5 g Proteins
12 g Fat
147 Cal.

Ingredients:

- Large eggs – 4
- Granulated stevia/Erythritol blend – .5 cup
- Sea salt – .125 tsp.
- Vanilla extract – 1 tsp.
- Pumpkin pie spice – 1 tsp.
- Butter/coconut oil/ghee – 4 tbsp.
- Pumpkin puree Canned or homemade – 1 tsp.
- Super-fine almond flour – .5 cup
- Recommended Size for the Cooker: 3-4-quarts
- Coconut cooking oil spray or butter for the pot

Direction

1 Take the butter out of the refrigerator to become room temperature. Lightly grease or spray the cooker.
2 Use a mixer to whisk the eggs – blending until smooth. Slowly, add the sweetener.
3 Blend in the vanilla extract and puree. Fold in the pie spice, salt, and almond flour. Mix everything well and add to the crockpot.
4 Secure the lid – with a paper towel between the top and the fixings to absorb moisture on top of the custard.
5 Cook for 2 to 2.75 hours on the low setting. When it's done, it will begin to pull away from the slow cooker. The center will be set.
6 Enjoy warm and top it off with garnishes as desired.

87. Chocolate Bonbons

Serves: 6
Nutrition Value per serving: -0- g Net Carbs
1 g Proteins
10 g Fat
100 Cal.

Ingredients:

- Butter – 5 tbsp.
- Coconut oil – 3 tbsp.
- Sugar-free raspberry syrup – 2 tbsp.
- Cocoa powder – 2 tbsp.

Direction

1 Mix the entire batch of ingredients in a pan.
2 Empty the bombs into six molds or muffin tins.
3 Place the prepared tin into the freezer for a minimum of two hours. Enjoy!

Chocolate Coconut Bites

Serves: 6

Nutrition Value per serving:
9 g Net Carbs
9 g Proteins
27 g Fat
326 Cal.

Ingredients:

- Unsweetened 80% or higher dark chocolate – 4 oz.
- Heavy cream – .33 cup
- Coconut flour – 1 cup
- Chocolate protein powder – 1 tbsp.
- Shredded unsweetened coconut – .25 cup
- Coconut oil – 4 tbsp.

Direction

1. Dice the dark chocolate into bits.
2. Warm up the heavy cream in a saucepan med-low. Stir in the chocolate bits and oil. Continue stirring until combined and remove from the burner.
3. Stir in the protein powder and coconut flour. Store in the refrigerator for a minimum of two hours.
4. Take the dough out of the fridge when they are cool. Shape into balls and roll through the shredded coconut until coated.
5. Store in the fridge in a closed container.

88. Chocolate Covered Almonds

Serves: 1
Nutrition Value per serving: 3 g Net Carbs
4 g Proteins
15 g Fat
183 Cal.

Ingredients:

- Unsweetened dark chocolate baking chips – .75 cup
- Whole raw almonds – 1.5 cups
- Pure vanilla extract – 1 tsp.
- Sea salt – 1 pinch

Direction

1. Cut a piece of parchment paper and cover a baking tray.
2. Toss the chips into a saucepan using low heat. Stir and add the vanilla.
3. Once the chocolate is melted, add the almonds and stir until coated.
4. Arrange them on the baking tin and dust with the salt.
5. Place in the fridge for a minimum of 30 minutes before you are ready to devour your portion.
6. For a taste change, sprinkle with some ground cinnamon.

89. Coconut Peanut Butter Balls

Serves: 15
Nutrition Value per serving: 0.92 g Net Carbs
0.98 g Proteins
3.19 g Fat
35.1 Cal.

Ingredients:

- Creamy peanut butter – Keto-friendly – 3 tbsp.
- Powdered Erythritol – 2.5 tsp.
- Unsweetened cocoa powder – 3 tsp.
- Almond flour – 2 tsp.
- Unsweetened coconut flakes – .5 cup

Direction

1 Combine the peanut butter, Erythritol, cocoa, and flour. Place in the freezer for one hour.
2 Spoon out a small spoon size of the butter mix. Roll into the flakes until it is covered.
3 Refrigerate overnight for the best results and enjoy.

90. Cheesecake Cupcakes

Serves: 12
Nutrition Value per serving: 2.1 g Net Carbs
4.9 g Proteins
20 g Fat
204 Cal.

Ingredients:

- Butter – .25 cup – melted
- Almond meal – .5 cup
- Eggs – 2
- Softened cream cheese – 16 oz. pkg.
- Stevia or your favorite sweetener – .75 cup
- Vanilla extract – 1 tsp.

Direction

1 Warm up the oven until it reaches 350ºF. Prepare a muffin tin with 12 paper liners.
2 Combine the butter and almond meal. Spoon into the cups to make a flat crust.
3 Whisk the vanilla, sweetener of choice, eggs, and cream cheese with an electric mixer until creamy. Scoop it in on top of the crust. Bake for 15-17 minutes.
4 Once they're done the cooking cycle, just remove and cool at room temperature. Store overnight or at least 8 hours.
5 Enjoy anytime for a delicious treat.

91. Individual Strawberry Cheesecakes

Serves: 4
Nutrition Value per serving: 9 g Net Carbs
8 g Proteins
47 g Fat
489 Cal.

Ingredients for the Crust

- Almond flour – .5 cup
- Melted butter/coconut oil – 3 tbsp.
- Sugar substitute – your preference – .25 cup or Maple syrup

Ingredients for the Filling:

- Sugar substitute – 3 tbsp. or use Grade B maple syrup
- Strawberries – 6
- Cream cheese – 8 oz.
- Sour cream – .33 cup
- Pure vanilla extract – .5 tsp.

Ingredients for the Garnish

- Strawberries – 4
- Fresh mint leaves

Direction

1 Combine the crust fixings in a mixing bowl. Blend well and divide into four small ramekins. Gently press

with your fingers.

2 Prepare the filling in a food processor. Pulse until creamy smooth.
3 Divide it over the crust of each one and chill for an hour or until it’s set.
4 Garnish with another berry if desired and serve. Add the carbs for any added garnishes

92. Lemon Mousse Cheesecake

Serves: 1
Nutrition Value per serving: 1.7 g Net Carbs
3.7 g Proteins
30 g Fat
277 Cal.

Ingredients:

- Lemon juice – 2 lemons approx. – .25 cup
- Cream cheese – 8 oz.
- Salt – .125 tsp.
- Lemon liquid Stevia – 1 tsp. or to your liking
- Heavy cream – 1 cup

Direction

1 Use a mixer to blend the lemon juice and cream cheese until it's creamy smooth. Add the remainder of the ingredients and whip until blended.
2 Taste test. Add to a serving dish and sprinkle with some lemon zest.
3 Refrigerate until you are ready to enjoy.

93. New York Cheesecake Cupcakes

Serves: 12
Nutrition Value per serving: 14.7 g Net Carbs
6.5g Proteins
26.7 g Fat
273 Cal.

Ingredients:

- Melted butter – 5 tbsp.
- Almond meal – .66 cup
- Cream cheese – 16 oz.
- Sour cream – .5 cup
- Swerve or another favorite – .75 cup
- Water – 2 tbsp.
- Heavy whipping cream – .25 cup
- Eggs -3
- Almond flour – 2 tbsp.
- Vanilla extract – 1.5 tsp.

Direction

1 Heat up the oven to reach 350°F. Prepare a 12-count muffin pan with paper liners.
2 Combine the butter and almond meal and spoon into the liners to form the crust.
3 Stir the sweetener and cream cheese until creamy. Blend in with the water and whipping cream. One at a time, add the eggs, stirring with each one.
4 Next, fold in the flour, sour cream, and extract. Spoon into the liners.
5 Bake for 15-18 minutes. Don't over-cook. The middle will be set when it's done. Cool on the countertop until room temperature. Then, store in the fridge overnight or a minimum of 8 hours.

94. Plain Cheesecake – No Bake

Serves: 6
Nutrition Value per serving: 5 g Net Carbs
6.9 g Proteins
25 g Fat
247 Cal.

Ingredients for the Crust:

- Melted coconut oil – 2 tbsp.
- Almond flour – 2 tbsp.
- Swerve Confectioner's/equivalent – 2 tbsp.
- Crushed salted almonds – 2 tbsp.

Filling Ingredients:

- Swerve confectioner's/equivalent – .25 cup
- Gelatin – 1 tsp.
- Cream cheese – 16 oz. pkg.
- Unsweetened almond milk – .5 cup
- Vanilla extract – 1 tsp.

Direction

1. Prepare the crust by combining all of the fixings under the crust section. Place one heaping tablespoon into the bottom of dessert cups. Press the mixture down and set aside.
2. Prepare the filling. Mix the sweetener and gelatin. Pour in the milk and stir 5 min.. Whip the vanilla beans and cream cheese with a mixer on medium until creamy. Add the gelatin mixture slowly until well incorporated.
3. Pour the mixture over the crust of each cup. Chill for three hours, minimum.

Appetizer & Snacks

95. Lamb & Leek Burgers with Lemon Cream

Serves: 4 burgers.

Prep Time: 25 minutes

Nutrition Value per serving:

Calories: 170 Cal, Carbs: 1.6 g, Net Carbs: 0.6 g, Fat: 8 g, Protein: 23 g, Fiber: 1 g.

Ingredients:

- 16-ounce ground lamb
- large lettuce leaves
- 1/2 cup chopped leeks
- 1/2 tablespoon garlic powder
- 1/2 teaspoon sea salt
- 1 tablespoon lemon zest
- 1 tablespoon coconut oil
- ½ cup coconut cream

Directions

1 Place a skillet pan over medium heat, add ½ teaspoon oil and when heated, add leeks.

2 Let cook for 3 to 5 minutes or until softened, then transfer to a bowl and let cool at room temperature.

3 Place ground meat in another bowl and add garlic powder and salt.

4 Add cooled leeks and mix until combined.
5 The shaped mixture into four patties.
6 Return skillet over medium-low heat, add remaining oil and add patties in it.
7 Let cook for 5 minutes per side or until cooked through.
8 In the meantime, place coconut cream and lemon zest in a blender and pulse until combined.
9 Place each patty in a large lettuce leaf, top with prepared cream dressing, then fold and serve.

96. Salmon Stuffed Avocado

Serves: 2.

Prep Time: 40 minutes

Nutrition Value per serving:

Calories: 463 Cal, Carbs: 13.9 g, Net Carbs: 6.4 g, Fat: 34.6 g, Protein: 27 g, Fiber: 7.5 g.

Ingredients:

- 8-ounce salmon fillets, cooked
- 1 large avocado, cored
- 1 tablespoon chopped dill
- 1 small white onion, peeled and chopped
- ¾ teaspoon salt
- ½ teaspoon ground black pepper
- tablespoons lemon juice
- 1 tablespoon coconut oil
- 1/4 cup soured cream
- lemon wedges for garnish

Directions

1 Set oven to 400 degrees F and let preheat.

2 In the meantime, take a baking tray, line with parchment sheet and place salmon fillets on it.

3 Drizzle with coconut oil and 1 tablespoon lemon juice and season with salt and black pepper.

4 Place the baking tray into the oven and let bake for

25 minutes or until cooked through.

5 When done, remove salmon from oven, let cool for 10 minutes and then shred using a fork, discarding skin.
6 Place shredded salmon in a bowl and add onion, cream, dill and lemon juice.
7 Stir until combined and then taste to adjust salt and black pepper.
8 Cut avocado into half, remove its pit and then scoop out about 1-inch avocado flesh using an ice cream scoop.
9 Cut scoop out avocado into small pieces, add to salmon mixture, stir until mixed and then fill prepared salmon mixture into that hollow.
10 Drizzle with lemon juice and serve.

97. Smoked Salmon Appetizer

Serves: 6.

Prep Time: 20 minutes

Nutrition Value per serving:

Calories: 330 Cal, Carbs: 3 g, Net Carbs: 3 g, Fat: 26 g, Protein: 23 g, Fiber: 0 g.

Ingredients:

- 7-ounce smoked salmon
- 2-ounce small lettuce leaves
- ¼ teaspoon ground black pepper
- tablespoons chopped dill
- tablespoons lemon zest
- 8-ounce cream cheese
- 15 teaspoon sour cream

Directions

1 Cut salmon into small even pieces and then place in a large bowl.

2 Add remaining ingredients to a bowl except for lettuce and stir until well mixed.

3 Let this mixture sit for 15 minutes.

4 Then fill lettuce leaves with the prepared salmon mixture and serve.

98. Roasted Cauliflower Hummus

Serves: 4.

Prep Time: 55 minutes

Nutrition Value per serving:

Calories: 40 Cal, Carbs: 2 g, Net Carbs: 1 g, Fat: 4 g, Protein: 1 g, Fiber: 1 g.

Ingredients:

- 1 medium-sized head of cauliflower
- 1 clove of garlic, peeled
- 1 lemon, cut into wedges
- tablespoons chopped parsley
- 1 teaspoon salt
- ¾ teaspoon ground black pepper
- 1/3 cup tahini paste
- tablespoons lemon juice
- tablespoons olive oil, divided
- Vegetable slices for serving

Directions

1 Set oven to 400 degrees F and let preheat.

2 Take a large rimmed baking sheet, grease with non-stick

cooking spray.

3 Cut cauliflower into florets and then arrange on a baking sheet in a single layer.
4 Drizzle with 2 tablespoons oil and then place baking sheet into the oven.
5 Let bake for 40 minutes or until roasted, stirring halfway through.
6 When done, remove baking sheet from oven and let cool on wire rack.
7 Then transfer cauliflower florets in a food processor and add garlic, salt, black pepper, tahini paste, lemon juice and olive oil.
8 Pulse for 2 minutes or until smooth and tip hummus in a bowl.
9 Drizzle with olive oil, sprinkle with parsley and serve with lemon wedges and vegetable slices.

99. Brussels Sprout Chips

Serves: 3.
Prep Time: 30 minutes

Nutrition Value per serving:

Calories: 296 Cal, Carbs: 12 g, Net Carbs: 8 g, Fat: 28 g, Protein: 4 g, Fiber: 4 g.

Ingredients:

- 8-ounce Brussels sprouts, thinly sliced
- 1 teaspoon garlic powder
- 1 teaspoon salt
- ¾ teaspoon ground black pepper
- 1 tablespoon olive oil
- tablespoons grated Parmesan cheese

Directions

1. Set oven to 400 degrees F and let preheat.
2. Place slices of Brussels sprouts in a large bowl and drizzle with olive oil.
3. Add garlic powder, salt, black pepper and cheese and toss to evenly coat.
4. Spread Brussels sprouts in a single layer on a baking sheet and then place into the oven.
5. Let bake for 20 minutes, tossing halfway through, until nicely golden brown and crispy.
6. Serve with your favorite dipping sauce.

100. Cream Cheese Stuffed Peppers

Serves: 8 bell peppers.
Prep Time: 30 minutes

Nutrition Value per serving:

Calories: 410 Cal, Carbs: 7 g, Net Carbs: 6 g, Fat: 37 g, Protein: 12 g, Fiber: 1 g.

Ingredients:

- 8-ounce small-sized bell peppers
- 1-ounce chorizo, chopped
- 1 tablespoon chopped cilantro
- 1 tablespoon chipotle paste
- tablespoons olive oil
- 8-ounce cream cheese
- 1 cup grated parmesan cheese

Directions

1 Set oven to 400 degrees F and let preheat.
2 In the meantime, cut each bell pepper into half, lengthwise, and then remove its core.
3 Stir together all the ingredients except for parmesan cheese and then fill into peppers.
4 Take a baking sheet, line with non-stick cooking spray and place stuffed peppers on it.
5 Spread cheese onto each pepper and let bake for 15 to 20 minutes or until cheese melts and the top is nicely golden brown.

Soups, Broth & Stews

101. Dill Pickle Soup

Serves: 8

Nutritional values per serving:

Calories – 517.5, Fat – 49.83 g, Total Carbohydrate – 4.77 g, Net Carbohydrate – 3.94 g, Fiber – 0.83 g, Protein – 14.09 g

Ingredients

- 2 tablespoons butter
- 2 teaspoons dried parsley
- 1 small onion, chopped
- 1 cup dill pickle juice
- 6.3 ounces dill pickle, finely chopped
- ½ cup chicken broth
- 6 tablespoons olive oil
- 1 cup bacon, cooked, crumbled
- 2 teaspoons garlic, minced
- 2 stalks celery, chopped
- 2 cups heavy whipping cream
- 1 cup xanthan gum
- 1 cup Cheddar cheese, shredded

Direction

1. Place a soup pot over medium heat. Add butter. When butter melts, add garlic and sauté for a few seconds until fragrant.
2. Stir in the parsley, onions, celery and chopped dill pickle. Cook for 5 minutes.
3. Add broth, pickle juice and cream.
4. When it begins to boil, add olive oil and xanthan gum into a bowl and whisk well. Add into the pot. Stir constantly until the soup is thick.
5. Add bacon and Cheddar cheese and stir.
6. Ladle into soup bowls and serve.

102. Dairy Free Cream of Chicken Soup

Serves: 4

Nutritional values per serving:

Calories – 198, Fat – 6.9 g, Total Carbohydrate – 9.4 g, Net Carbohydrate – 5.6 g, Fiber – 3.8 g, Protein – 26.4 g

Ingredients

- 2 medium cauliflowers, cut into florets
- 2 cups chicken broth
- 1 teaspoon grey sea salt
- Freshly ground pepper to taste
- ¼ teaspoon dried thyme
- ½ cup chicken thighs, cooked, finely chopped
- 1 1/3 cups almond milk, unsweetened
- 2 teaspoons onion powder
- ½ teaspoon garlic powder
- ¼ teaspoon celery seeds optional
- ½ cup Collagen protein beef gelatin optional

Direction

1. Gather all the ingredients. Add all the ingredients except chicken and gelatin into a soup pot.
2. Place the soup pot over medium heat. Cover with a lid.
3. When it begins to boil, lower heat and simmer until cauliflower is tender.
4. Turn off the heat. Take out about a cup of the cooked liquid and add into a bowl.
5. Add gelatin, a little at a time into the bowl of cooked liquid. Whisk well each time. The gelatin should dissolve completely.
6. Pour the gelatin mixture into a blender. Add cauliflower mixture.
7. Blend until smooth and creamy.
8. Pour the soup back into the pot. Place the pot over low heat.
9. Add chicken and stir. Cover and cook until the soup is heated thoroughly.
10. Ladle into soup bowls and serve.

103. Tomato Asiago Soup

Serves: 8

Nutritional values per serving:

Calories – 301.5, Fat – 25.79 g, Total Carbohydrate – 10.72 g, Net Carbohydrate – 8.75 g, Fiber – 1.98 g, Protein – 9.29 g

Ingredients

- 2 cans tomato paste
- 1 ½ cups Asiago cheese, shredded
- 2 teaspoons dried oregano
- Salt to taste
- Pepper powder to taste
- 2 cups heavy whipping cream
- ½ cup water
- 2 teaspoons garlic, minced

Direction

1. Place a soup pot over medium heat. Add tomato paste, garlic and onion. Mix well.
2. Add cream and whisk well.
3. When it begins to boil, add cheese, a little at a time and whisk well each time.
4. Add water and let it boil for about 5 minutes.
5. Ladle into soup bowls. Sprinkle pepper on top and serve.

104. Roasted Poblano and Cheddar Soup

Serves: 8

Nutritional values per serving:

Calories – 241.5, Fat – 16.88 g, Total Carbohydrate – 14.39 g, Net Carbohydrate – 10.41 g, Fiber – 3.98 g, Protein – 10.66 g

Ingredients

- 4 medium poblano peppers
- 5 cups vegetable stock
- ½ cup sour cream
- 2 tablespoons garlic powder
- 2 teaspoons smoked paprika
- 1 medium cauliflower, cut into florets
- 2 tablespoons butter
- 2 ¼ cups Cheddar cheese, shredded
- 2 teaspoons cumin powder
- ½ cup onion, chopped

Direction

1. Preheat the broiler to high setting.
2. Place poblano peppers on a baking sheet.
3. Broil in the oven until tender and the skin is slightly charred.
4. Remove the peppers from the oven and transfer

into a bowl. Cover with a lid and let it cool. Discard the skin and seeds and chop pepper into small pieces. Set aside.

5. In the meantime keep the cauliflower florets in a bowl and microwave for 5-6 minutes or until tender.
6. Cool slightly and transfer into a blender. Add a little stock and blend until smooth. Add remaining stock and blend until well combined.
7. Place a soup pot over medium heat. Add butter. When butter melts, add onions and sauté until translucent.
8. Add rest of the ingredients into the soup pot and stir until well combined.
9. When it begins to boil, retain a little of the pepper for garnishing and add rest into the pot. Let it simmer for 5-6 minutes.
10. Ladle into soup bowls. Sprinkle retained pepper on top and serve.

105. Spring Soup

Serves: 4

Nutritional values per serving:

Calories – 150, Fat – 5 g, Total Carbohydrate – 11 g, Net Carbohydrate – 4 g, Fiber – 7 g, Protein – 16 g

Ingredients

- 4 eggs
- 2 heads romaine lettuce, chopped
- 2 quarts chicken broth
- Salt to taste

Direction

1. Pour broth into a large saucepan. Place the saucepan over medium heat.
2. When it begins to boil, lower the heat.
3. Crack one egg at a time into a bowl and slide it gently into the simmering broth.
4. Simmer for 5 minutes. Carefully remove the egg and place into soup bowls.
5. Add lettuce into the simmering broth and cook until it wilts.
6. Ladle soup into the bowls over the eggs and serve.

106. Kale and Sausage Soup

Serves: 3

Nutritional values per serving:

Calories – 298, Fat – 24 g, Total Carbohydrate – 8.49 g, Net Carbohydrate – 6 g, Fiber – 2.49 g, Protein – 16 g

Ingredients

- ½ pound ground sweet Italian sausage
- 1 small yellow onion, chopped
- 1 clove garlic, crushed
- 1 small carrot, peeled, diced
- ½ small head cauliflower, broken into florets
- 1 ½ cups kale, discard hard stems and ribs, chopped
- 2 teaspoons butter
- 1 tablespoon red wine vinegar
- ½ teaspoon dried rubbed sage
- ½ teaspoon dried oregano
- ½ teaspoon crushed red pepper flakes or to taste
- ½ teaspoons dried basil
- 2 cups low sodium chicken broth
- Freshly ground pepper to taste
- Salt to taste
- ½ cup heavy cream

Direction

1. Place a soup pot over medium high heat. Add sausage. Cook until brown. Break it simultaneously as it cooks.
2. Remove with a slotted spoon and place on a plate that is lined with paper towels.
3. Discard the excess fat from the pot.
4. Place the pot back over medium heat.
5. Add onion and carrots and sauté until onions are translucent.
6. Add garlic and cook for a minute. Add vinegar and scrape the bottom of the pot to remove any brown bits that are stuck.
7. Add spices, herbs, stock and cream and stir.
8. When it begins to boil, add cauliflower and stir.
9. Lower the heat and simmer until cauliflower is tender.
10. Add kale and sausage. Mix well. Cook until kale wilts. Add salt and pepper and stir.
11. Ladle into soup bowls and serve.

107. Hot Chili Soup

Serves: 8

Nutritional values per serving:

Calories – 369.5, Fat – 25.86 g, Total Carbohydrate – 10.17 g, Net Carbohydrate – 6.44 g, Fiber – 3.73 g, Protein – 27.03 g

Ingredients

- 2 teaspoons coriander seeds
- 4 medium chili peppers, sliced
- 4 cups water
- 2 pounds chicken thighs
- 4 cups chicken broth
- 4 tablespoons olive oil
- 3 tablespoons butter
- 8 tablespoons tomato paste
- 1 teaspoon ground turmeric
- 1 large avocado, peeled, pitted, sliced
- 4 chili peppers sliced or to taste
- 1 ½ teaspoons ground cumin
- 4 ounces queso fresco cheese
- 4 tablespoons lime juice
- Salt to taste
- Pepper powder to taste

Direction

1. Place a soup pot over medium heat. Add a little oil. When the oil is heated, add chicken. Cook until chicken is tender. Place chicken thighs in soup bowls.

2. Add remaining oil. When oil is heated, add coriander seeds and sauté for a few seconds until fragrant.

3. Add chili pepper and sauté for a few seconds. Add salt, pepper, turmeric and ground cumin. Add water and allow it to boil.

4. Reduce heat and let it simmer for a few minutes. Add tomato paste and butter and continue simmering for another 10 minutes. Turn off the heat.

5. Ladle soup over chicken.

6. Place a few slices of avocado in each bowl, a little queso fresco cheese and cilantro and serve.

108. Asparagus Soup

Serves: 6

Prep Time: 1 hour and 10 minutes

Ingredients:

- tablespoons ghee
- 1 white onion, chopped
- cloves garlic, crushed
- cups chicken broth
- 1 cup ham, diced
- lb. asparagus, sliced in half
- ½ teaspoon dried thyme
- Salt and pepper to taste

Directions:

1 Select the sauté function in the Instant Pot.

2 Add the ghee.

3 Add the onion and cook for 5 minutes.

4 Add the garlic, broth and ham.

5 Simmer for 3 minutes.

6 Add the asparagus and thyme.

7 Secure the pot.

8 Choose soup setting.

9 Cook for 45 minutes.

10 Blend the mixture in a food processor.

11 Season with the salt and pepper.

Serving Suggestion: Garnish with low-carb croutons.

Tip: You can also use an immersion blender instead of a food processor.

Nutritional Information Per Serving:
Calories160

Total Fat 13.4g

Saturated Fat 7.9g

Cholesterol 29mg

Sodium 807mg

Total Carbohydrate 6.9g

Dietary Fiber 4g

Total Sugars 4.1g

Protein 10.7g

109. Carrot Soup

Serves: 4

Prep Time: 20 minutes

Ingredients:

- ½ onion, diced
- 1 clove garlic, minced
- carrots, sliced into cubes
- cups vegetable broth
- 15 oz. coconut milk
- Salt and pepper to taste

Directions:

1 Press the sauté button in the Instant Pot.

2 Add the oil.

3 Sauté onion and garlic for 1-3 minutes.

4 Add the carrots, vegetable broth and coconut milk.

5 Season with the salt and pepper.

6 Seal the pot.

7 Choose manual mode.

8 Cook at high pressure for 8 minutes.

9 Release the pressure naturally.

10 Use an immersion blender to blend the soup until smooth.

Serving Suggestion: Serve this soup with coconut cream and top with chopped parsley.

Tip: You can also use a regular blender to blend the soup.

Nutritional Information Per Serving:
Calories320

Total Fat 26g

Saturated Fat 22.7g

Cholesterol 0mg

Sodium 482mg

Total Carbohydrate 19.9g

Dietary Fiber 5.7g

Total Sugars 10.5g

Protein 6.1g

Potassium 796mg

110. Spring Keto Stew with Venison

Serves: 2
Prep Time: 20 minutes

Ingredients:

- 1 lb venison stew meat
- 1/2 cup purple cabbage, shredded
- 1/2 cup celery, sliced
- cup bone broth
- Directions
- Sauté cabbage and celery with olive oil and garlic in a skillet.
- Add the venison and season with salt and pepper to taste. Stir until meat is browned.
- Transfer everything into the crockpot. Add the cone broth.
- Cover and cook on low for 6 hours.

Nutrition Value per serving:
Calories: 310, Fat: 16 g, Net carbs: 5 g, Protein: 32 g

Serving suggestions: When cooked, add the asparagus for extra flavor and greens. Serve with lime if desired.

111. Mexican Taco Soup

Serves: 2
Prep Time: 5 minutes

Ingredients:

- 1 lb ground meat, browned
- oz cream cheese
- oz diced tomatoes and chilis
- 1 tbsp of taco seasonings
- 1 cup of chicken broth
- Directions
- Combine all ingredients in the crockpot.
- Cook on low for 4 hours.

Nutrition Value per serving:
Calories: 547, Fat: 43 g, Net carbs: 5 g, Protein: 33 g

Serving suggestions: Stir in cilantro or garnish with shredded cheese before serving.

112. Oxtail Stew

Serves: 2
Prep Time: 20 minutes

Ingredients:

- lb oxtail, chopped
- tomatoes, diced
- tsp paprika
- Directions
- Place oxtail in the crockpot with water filling up to half the pot.
- Cover and cook for 10 hours on low.
- When cooked, transfer the oxtail to a saucepan and add the tomatoes paprika and other desired seasonings garlic cloves, chili powder, salt.
- Stew for 15 minutes.

Nutrition Value per serving:
Calories: 456, Fat: 29 g, Net carbs: 7 g, Protein: 37 g

113. Rabbit Stew

Serves: 2
Prep Time: 20 minutes

Ingredients:

- 1 rabbit, browned
- 1 lb andouille sausage, cut to 1/2 inches thick
- medium carrots, 1-inch chunks
- qt chicken stock
- Spices of choice
- Directions
- Sauté onion, sausage and desired spices in a skillet, then add half of the stock to deglaze.
- Put the rabbit in the crockpot and add the contents of the skillet.
- Cover and cook for 6 hours on high.

Nutrition Value per serving:
Calories: 381, Fat: 32 g, Net carbs: 4 g, Protein: 29 g

Tip: You can add mushrooms for extra flavor.

114. Rosemary Turkey and Kale Soup

Serves: 2
Prep Time: 20 minutes

Ingredients:

- carrots, sliced
- cups turkey stock
- 1 sprig rosemary
- cups turkey meat, bite-size pieces
- cups kale, chopped

Directions

1 Sauté onion, carrots and desired spices in a skillet, then add half of the stock to deglaze.
2 Put the turkey in the crockpot and add the contents of the skillet.
3 Cover and cook for 8 hours on low.
4 Add the kale when cooked.

Nutrition Value per serving:
Calories: 403, Fat: 28 g, Net carbs: 6 g, Protein: 34 g

Serving suggestions: Remove the turkey rosemary before serving.

Tip: If the soup is to be served later, do not add the kale until just before serving.

Conclusion

Thanks for downloading this book. It's my firm belief that it will provide you with all the answers to your questions.

Made in the USA
San Bernardino, CA
22 April 2019